CREATIVE CLAY
JEWELRY

CREATIVE CLAY JEWELRY

Extraordinary ⋄ *Colorful* ⋄ *Fun*

DESIGNS TO MAKE FROM POLYMER CLAY

LESLIE DIERKS

Lark Books

Published in 1994 by Lark Books
50 College Street
Asheville, North Carolina, U.S.A., 28801

© 1994 by Lark Books

Design: Kathleen Holmes
Photography: Evan Bracken
Illustrations: Orrin Lundgren
Handmade papers: Susan Kinney
Production: Elaine Thompson, Kathleen Holmes

ISBN 0-937274-74-7

Library of Congress Cataloging in Publication Data
Dierks, Leslie.
　　Creative clay jewelry : extraordinary, colorful, fun designs to make
　from polymer clay / Leslie Dierks.
　　　　p.　cm.
　　Includes bibliographical references and index.
　　ISBN 0-937274-74-7
　　1. Plastics craft.　2. Jewelry making.　I. Title
TT297.D54　1994
745.594'2–dc20　　　　　　　　　　　　　　　　93-37188
　　　　　　　　　　　　　　　　　　　　　　　　CIP

10 9 8 7 6 5 4

Printed in Hong Kong by Oceanic Graphic Printing

*Page 2: A multi-strand necklace in classic black and white
by Tamela Wells.*

Page 3: "Log Cabin" quilt square pin by Diane Keeler.

*Opposite: Yin and yang necklace by Janet Kruk, Aaron
Larson, and Josue Peters.*

CONTENTS

CONTRIBUTING ARTISTS

BRIDGET ALBANO began working in polymer clay six years ago, first as a hobby, then as a full-time artist. When not making jewelry at her studio, Exclaymation!, in Claymont, Delaware, she can often be found teaching classes on polymer clay. (Pages 20, 64, 97, 118)

An artist of many talents, **KATHLEEN AMT** has worked and taught in metals, ceramics, and fiber in addition to polymer clay. She markets her work through the Torpedo Factory in Alexandria, Virginia or from her studio in Mt. Rainier, Maryland. (Pages 19, 113, 131, 144)

SUE BALESTRERI's enjoyment of the precision and absorption required for beadwork, specifically constructing earrings from seed beads, and for making Ukrainian eggs led to her discovery of polymer clay. She lives and works in Tucson, Arizona, where she exhibits her work in selected craft shows. (Page 82)

In addition to making jewelry and practicing nursing, **THESSALY BARNETT** is an avid teacher. For ten years she has taught classes in woven neck pieces, bead stringing, paper jewelry, and polymer clay. A resident of Oakland, California, she currently sells her work through local boutiques. (Pages 20, 105, 128)

LORI BARTHOLOMEW derives her inspiration mainly from the natural beauty that surrounds her home and studio in Canton, North Carolina. Under the professional name Lori Ann, she exhibits her

Two tourists enjoy the sights in this pin by Marguerite Kuhl and Jane Vislocky.

hand sculpted jewelry at regional craft shows. (Pages 111, 121)

MAUREEN CARLSON's unlimited imagination is applied to creating a world full of delightful characters through her business, Wee Folk Creations in Prior Lake, Minnesota. She has recently introduced a line of press molds called "What a Character," which can be used to mold a variety of human faces with polymer clay. (Pages 31, 32, 116)

CLAIRE LATIES DAVIS is a graduate of Rhode Island School of Design, where she studied jewelry and metal working. Her distinctive painterly style of working with polymer clay developed from her efforts to add color to her work using a non-toxic material. Her studio, Runes Designs, is located in Edgewood, Rhode Island. (Pages 19, 98, 100)

IRENE DEAN is a polymer clay artist and instructor who lives in Weaverville, North Carolina. Although she has experimented with a number of techniques, she finds canework the most fascinating. She markets her work directly from her studio, good night irene!, and at local shows and area shops. (Pages 37, 39, 40, 42, 44)

KATHLEEN DUSTIN has worked in ceramics and polymer clay since 1975 and is one of the first to teach millefiore workshops. Her recent years in Turkey have inspired designs rich in color and liberal in their use of gold leaf. She markets her work directly from her Houston, Texas, studio and through galleries and craft shows. (Page 139)

With a background in architecture, where projects require months or years to complete, **LORETTA ANNE FONTAINE** takes great pleasure from the immediacy of polymer clay. She lives and works in Albany, New York, and her jewelry can be found in select upstate New York galleries. (Pages 52, 88, 95)

STEVEN FORD and **DAVID FORLANO** are the owners of City Zen Cane in Philadelphia, Pennsylvania. For six years the two have collaborated on polymer clay designs, most notably their trademarked series of tube images. These designs fool the eye with their three-dimensional effects. (Pages 9, 17, 26, 92)

MYRNA KANTER has crafted polymer clay jewelry in her studio in New York City for about five years. Through the classes she teaches locally, she shares the techniques for making the colorful millefiore patterns that fill her pieces, and she displays her work at craft fairs and shows. (Pages 54, 69)

DIANE KEELER's primary interest in polymer clay is expressed in her clay figures, whose every feature, including their clothing, is made of polymer clay. She also makes large dolls. Her jewelry developed from the quilt squares she made to adorn her sculptures, and they reflect her whimsical nature. (Pages 3, 79)

Having lived in Japan and Hawaii for a number of years, **SUSAN KINNEY** has been strongly influenced by oriental art. In addition to creating polymer clay jewelry that is sold in galleries across the U.S., she is a potter and interior designer. Her studio, Suezen, is located in Asheville, North Carolina. (Pages 16, 86, 107, 130)

JANET KRUK, **AARON LARSON**, and **JOSUE PETERS** combine their creative talents at Crooked-River Crafts in LaFarge, Wisconsin. Janet, whose background is in fine art and metal jewelry making, designs the overall compositions, and Aaron and Josh bring a youthful vitality to the design and execution of the component beads. (Pages 5, 48)

MARGUERITE KUHL and **JANE VISLOCKY** are both watercolor artists who have been soundly bitten by the polymer clay "bug." Their knowledge of the material is largely self-taught, and their passion for it

has led to a shared studio in Cocoa Beach, Florida, where they work together creating lots of fanciful jewelry and not so many watercolors. (Pages 6, 21, 30, 31, 72, 136, 143)

When presented with a design problem—what sort of "power" neckwear should the female executive wear—**PATRICIA KUTZA** established What Knot Accessories. Her mixed media designs have incorporated polymer clay since 1989. Her work has been the focus of a one-woman exhibit and is marketed from her studio in Alameda, California, and at shows throughout California. (Page 124)

All her life **NINA PICCIRILLI** has wanted to create imaginative little animals from clay. Zoolery, her studio in Ft. Lauderdale, Florida, is the fulfillment of that dream. Her animals are content to sit pinned to a jacket lapel or hat brim, and their whimsical spirit has spilled over into all of Nina's work. (Pages 17, 18, 20, 76)

ILEEN SHEFFERMAN brings her experience as a potter and jewelry designer to her polymer clay creations. A past president of the National Polymer Clay Guild, she also teaches classes in polymer clay. She displays her work at the Torpedo Factory in Alexandria, Virginia, and in area galleries and craft shops. (Page 108)

LYNNE SWARD is primarily a fiber artist who reclaims commercial fabrics, making them into wearable art, fabric collages, quilts, dolls, and mixed media sculptures. Her polymer clay jewelry, crafted in her studios in Virginia Beach, Virginia, reflects her love of fabric. (Pages 101, 103, 126)

TAMELA WELLS is a full-time polymer clay artist with a strong instinct for design and color. Working from her studio, Heartworks, in Asheville, North Carolina, she sells her work through a number of galleries and at craft shows. (Pages 2, 38, 46, 50, 58, 60, 74, 85, 94, 134, 138, 142)

LINDA WISEHEART combines the vivid colors of polymer clay with the soft sheen of sterling silver for the jewelry she designs and creates in her studio, Mycenae, in Maryville, Tennessee. She displays her work at area craft fairs and local galleries. (Pages 10, 61, 90)

INTRODUCTION

Jewelry making is a craft practically as old as humanity itself. Ever since our ancestors made their homes in caves, we have created and worn body ornaments. We've made jewelry to bring good fortune, to indicate social standing, or merely to express our personalities. Whatever its other purposes, jewelry has invariably brought pleasure to its creators and to those who wear it.

Through the ages, a variety of materials both ordinary and exotic have been used to make jewelry. None is more colorful or versatile than polymer clay. The term polymer clay sounds like something you'd find in a chemistry text, but in fact it is the general name for a class of modelling compounds initially developed for use by doll makers and miniaturists. Polymer clay is a relative newcomer as an artistic medium, but it has been quickly and warmly embraced by jewelry makers.

There's no doubt why this material is becoming so popular. It's easy to use—requiring the simplest of tools—and demands no extensive training or highly developed skills. The few basic techniques can be quickly learned. With a pair of hands, a few household items, and some imagination, you can create beautiful designs from polymer clay in a single afternoon. Then, after baking it in a low-temperature kitchen oven, the material hardens permanently and can be worn as jewelry.

Available in a rainbow of brilliant colors, polymer clay is a soft, pliable material that lends itself to a variety of techniques. It can be textured, sculpted, treated like paint, incised, and stamped. It can be rolled into a ball, flattened into a sheet, and extruded through a press. It is compatible with (and will often bond to) found objects and any other materials that can withstand the low baking temperature required to harden polymer clay. If desired, you can embellish it with metallic powders or composition "gold" leaf, colored pencils or chalk, or you can paint the hardened clay. Polymer clay can be made to imitate other materials such as stone, leather, or glass. Alternatively, you can create fanciful images and improbable combinations. You can even use it to transfer printed images.

In the pages that follow you'll be guided through the basic methods for handling polymer clay, the tools you'll need, and the techniques for creating a number of interesting patterns. You'll be inspired by some superlative works by contemporary artists, and you'll discover the extraordinary potential of polymer clay through the 48 projects that follow. Representing the work of more than two dozen artists, these projects walk you through the entire process, step by step.

Now settle down in a comfortable chair, unwrap some polymer clay, and let's get started!

Opposite: The unmistakable style of Steven Ford and David Forlano is displayed in this striking necklace.

THE BASICS

WHAT IS POLYMER CLAY?

Polymer clay isn't a true clay; it's produced in factories rather than scooped from the earth. Like natural clay, this material is quite malleable in its raw state and becomes hard and rigid after firing. The main difference is that polymer clay is a plastic. While the exact formula varies by manufacturer, all polymer clays are made from polyvinyl chloride (PVC). The PVC is mixed with a plasticizer, which adds flexibility, and with color pigments. When baked at the proper temperature, the particles of PVC polymerize—hence the name, polymer clay. In the language of nonchemists, they fuse together, making the finished product both sturdy and durable.

Several techniques were combined to make these pins by Linda Wiseheart.

Baking is an appropriate term for this material's firing process. Unlike ceramics, which require temperatures of 1000°F (538°C) or more, polymer clay is hardened in a conventional oven at temperatures ranging from 215 to 275°F (102 to 135°C).

Unlike natural clay and earlier varieties of modelling compounds, this material is available in a rainbow of bright colors, including some fluorescent and metallic shades. The color is in the material, not on it, and won't bleed when two pieces of clay are placed side by side. However, if you want to mix colors—and this is one of the most satisfying qualities of polymer clay—you can easily create new hues by blending two or more shades from a single manufacturer or by combining different brands.

One of the best qualities of this material is its predictability. Baking causes no shrinkage, and the colors don't fade. Because polymer clay is heat activated, it doesn't dry out under normal circumstances. Its shelf life is something on the order of two years, and this can be extended by storing your clay in a refrigerator or freezer.

After baking, polymer clay is quite hard and stable. If desired, it can be sanded or drilled, but you should be careful when handling thin sections. Polymer clay is not very flexible once fired and will break when bent. In other words, beads are fairly indestructible, but long, thin items such as pins may be somewhat fragile.

Polymer clay is sold in most craft shops and by mail order through a variety of art and craft suppliers. The standard size package—one block—weighs about two ounces (65 grams). There are several brands, and your choice of which to use may be decided by which ones you find most readily available. Most of the projects in this book use either FIMO or Sculpey III or a combination of the two. Other brands you may have available include Cernit, Pro-Mat, and Modello.

FIMO, Cernit, and Modello are all produced in Germany. FIMO was initially developed in the 1930s for use in doll making and is manufactured by Eberhard Faber. Distributed worldwide, it has the largest range of colors of any brand. Cernit is less readily available and is slightly more expensive. Produced by T & F Kunststoffe, Cernit is highly prized by contemporary doll makers for its porcelainlike finish. Modello is manufactured by Rudolph Reiser and is only sparsely available.

Sculpey III, produced in the United States by Polyform Products Company, evolved from a popular line of single-color modelling compounds that have been on the market since the late 1960s. The most recent member of the Sculpey family is Pro-Mat, a material formulated for higher strength and flexibility. Its color selection, while more limited than the other clays, includes some vivid neon shades.

GETTING STARTED

Selecting an assortment of colors is an enjoyable process, but nothing beats actually getting some clay in your hands and playing with it. Some people have even described the process as therapeutic because it is so relaxing to roll, squeeze, and smoosh the material into different shapes and forms.

Clean your hands well before you start because polymer clay is a magnet for dirt and dust. The clay itself will leave a residue on your skin, and it is best to wash your hands or wipe them with lotion and a paper towel before changing colors. For best results, handle your lightest colors first, and work your way to the darkest ones. Red is particularly notorious for sticking to your fingers and staining other colors.

Workability of the material varies according to brand, and all polymer clays require some amount of conditioning to get them to their optimal consistency. This is done by taking a small portion of clay—no more than about one-eighth of a block— and working it in your hands. Your aim is to condition the material evenly, and this is easier if you work with small pieces at a time. Pinch the clay, roll it into a ball, flatten it into a sheet, and form it into a log. The warmth of your hands combined with the kneading process will actually change the consistency of the clay. Once it is soft and pliable and no longer tears when you stretch and bend it sharply, the material is ready to use.

Some brands of clay require more conditioning than others. Although the manufacturers have taken steps to soften the consistency of the stiffer clays (FIMO and Pro-Mat), some tips for dealing with a less yielding material may be helpful. First, try prewarming it before kneading. One approach is to put your clay in a plastic bag and carry it in your pocket or sit on it for a while. Alternatively, you can place it under a warm heating pad. Be careful with the heat setting, though; should your clay get much above body temperature, it can start to harden. If the material still doesn't feel comfortable to you, you can add a few drops of mineral oil, a small dab of petroleum jelly, or one of the manufacturer's thinners, FIMO Mix Quick or Sculpey Diluent, to the clay. Some people use a thin coating of lotion on their hands to help soften the clay. Try not to add too much of any thinner, or your material will become gummy. If that happens, mix in some additional clay.

Mix two or more colors into marbled patterns, or blend them thoroughly to make custom hues.

For those who fall in love with this material and find themselves working with large quantities, a food processor can take some of the effort out of conditioning and mixing polymer clay. (It is also helpful for arthritis sufferers.) The compact models are longer lasting than the minichoppers, whose blades may strip or motors burn out. Again working from lightest colors to darkest, chop about one two-ounce (65 gram) block at a time, cutting it into small portions before placing it in the bowl. A few drops of your chosen thinner will help the mixing process.

Once used for polymer clay, your food processor should not be used again for food. The residue from the clay will permeate the blade mechanisms and the porous surface of the plastic bowl. If you don't want to buy an entire new machine for your craft, purchase a spare bowl and chopping blade.

MIXING COLORS

One of the greatest joys of this material is the infinite range of colors you can mix. Although the manufacturers pride themselves in the selections they offer, artists who work in polymer clay take equal pride in the unique color blends they concoct. You should note that many—if not most—of these custom hues come about by accident. And some, no matter how carefully you follow your original recipe, seem impossible to reproduce. This is because polymer clay, like fabric and yarn, varies slightly in color from batch to batch.

Experiment freely with your colors, and enjoy the process of discovery. If you are aiming for a specific hue, start with small amounts because it is easy to accumulate quite a lot of clay when you keep adding "just a little bit more" of one color or another. When mixing dark colors with light ones, keep in mind that the darker color generally predominates, sometimes

Arranged on a work surface are some examples of rolling tools: two types of brayers, a rolling pin, glass vase, and pasta machine. Next to the craft knife is an assortment of slicing blades (left to right): tissue slicing blade, single-edge razor blade, a wallpaper scraper blade, and a clay slicing tool.

to the near exclusion of the lighter one. It's much safer to add dark to light in little bits at a time.

To decrease the intensity of a color (i.e., for a more "watered down" effect), mix a small amount of the desired color with some translucent clay. By varying the proportions of color to translucent, you can achieve anything from a thin "wash" of color to a full, slightly porcelainlike tone. A thin layer of unmixed translucent clay can also be applied over another color in your piece for some interesting effects. After baking, the translucent clay is somewhat murky, but you can see the color underneath. However, don't expect to detect detailed patterns through a layer of translucent clay.

Because color is such a significant factor in jewelry made from polymer clay, your choices for which colors to place next to one another are equally important. Colors that look perfectly wonderful apart can look dreadful when placed in close proximity. Remember too that most jewelry is quite small. Subtle contrasting shades will not be nearly so obvious in your finished pieces as they are in raw form. And, as the impressionist painters so effectively demonstrated, small amounts of contrasting colors placed closely together tend to blend in the eye. Blue placed next to yellow creates the impression of green. What you don't want to create is the impression of mud.

There are numerous books and other resources available about color theory for those so inclined. If you have a knack for colors, or even if you don't, go with your instincts. You'll know in five minutes whether you need to alter your colors or your design to make an effective combination. You can learn a lot about colors and how they go together by just playing and experimenting.

MARBLEIZING COLORS

The end result of mixing two or more colors doesn't have to be a complete blend. It's fun to produce abstract mottled patterns in different color combinations. One approach is to take small pieces of several colors of clay and pack them into a ball. Form the ball into a log, twist the log, and roll it into a ball once more. Continue making the ball into a log into a ball until you have a marbled pattern you enjoy.

Another approach is to start with logs of two or more colors. Spiral these together, and roll the combination into a ball. Form the ball into a log into a ball until the pattern pleases you.

TOOLS AND EQUIPMENT

The tools you'll need for making polymer clay jewelry are few in number, low in cost, and not at all complicated. In most cases there are many options for accomplishing the same goal, and you can find most of what you'll need right in your own home.

The first of these is a normal oven. Polymer clay is baked at a relatively low temperature, just above the "keep warm" setting on most ovens. Since too low a temperature can result in fragile pieces and too high a heat can burn your clay (and create some nasty fumes, see *Safety,* below), it pays to check your oven's temperature throughout the baking cycle with an oven thermometer. If you don't feel comfortable baking plastic in your kitchen oven, look for a used toaster oven at a flea market or garage sale. These are less likely to be accurate in their temperature, however, so be sure to check yours with a thermometer before committing your hard work to it.

Your primary tools are your hands. With just a little practice, these can become remarkably adept at shaping small forms, rolling round balls, and forming logs of consistent diameters. Many people feel comfortable only when their hands are in direct contact with the material. Others prefer to wear disposable latex examination gloves (some drugstores carry them) to avoid leaving fingerprints in their designs and to keep any clay residue from clinging to their skin. You can always burnish away the fingerprints; base your decision whether or not to wear gloves on your own comfort.

To avoid imprinting a texture on your clay, choose a work surface that is both smooth and flat. A piece of glass or plexiglass is ideal because you can pick it up and put it out of the way when you need to set your projects aside. Artificial counter top materials such as Formica also work well, and a small shelf covered in this material makes a fine work surface. Don't do your projects on an unprotected wooden table, though; the unbaked clay can harm the finish. It can also soften and bond to some plastics. Some people like to use a piece of wax paper taped in place onto a smooth surface. This technique makes the finished piece easy to pick up and move.

For flattening clay into sheets, you'll need a rolling tool. A smooth, cylindrical water glass or vase works well, as does a rolling pin. Polymer clay can stick to a wooden roller such as a rolling pin or large dowel. To improve its usefulness, coat the wood with polyurethane. Alternatively, you can apply a light film of mineral oil to the roller. A stone rolling pin designed for making pastries has fewer problems with sticking. A brayer—a roller with a single handle attached—is great for flattening small sheets and for transforming a round log into a square. Brayers are made of wood, rubber, or plastic and are available in graphic arts supply stores. The plastic ones work best but are the most difficult to find.

The Rolls-Royce of rolling tools is the pasta machine. This limited-purpose kitchen tool becomes much more versatile when working with polymer clay. Using any one of several settings, you can crank out sheet after sheet, all with a uniform thickness. Use the thickest setting to assist the conditioning process or

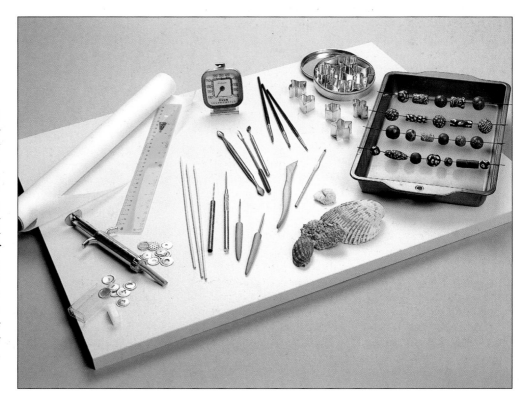

Other tools and equipment include (clockwise, starting at upper left): oven parchment paper, ruler, oven thermometer, paintbrushes, aspic cutters, a pan set up for baking beads, shells for adding texture, a variety of piercing tools, and a clay extruder with end plates. In the center are three jeweler's wax-working tools and other implements to manipulate clay.

for blending two colors together. Additionally, two or more colors passed through the rollers side by side can be bonded together to make a striped slab.

Again, if you requisition a pasta machine or any other tool from your kitchen to use with polymer clay, make sure the trip is one way. Consider these tools to be your sacrifice for your art; now relax and enjoy them.

A craft knife and one or more slicing blades are essential for working with polymer clay. You'll frequently want to cut shapes and trim sheets of clay, and for this purpose there is no tool better than a craft knife. To cut thin slices from the designs you construct, you'll need a long, thin, single-edge blade, the sharper the better. The blade from your craft knife or a single-edge razor blade can be used for smaller designs. A better alternative is a replacement blade for a wallpaper scraper (available at hardware or paint supply stores). A clay slicing tool (from a craft supply store) also works. For precision slicing, the tool beloved by professionals is the tissue-slicing blade. This is an exceedingly sharp blade sold by medical supply houses for use in pathology labs and other places you want to avoid.

If you plan to make beads, you'll also need a piercing tool. Tools designed specifically for this purpose are available commercially, but you can also use sewing needles, tapestry needles, darning needles, fine knitting needles, or wooden skewers.

Any number of other hand tools can be adapted for use with polymer clay. You can even construct your own by embedding a darning needle, fountain pen nib, or other object into a handle fashioned from polymer clay. After baking, both the tool and the rounded end of the handle can be used to create designs in your pieces. In addition to more conventional items such as jeweler's wax working tools, leather working tools, and wooden tools for clay sculpting, seek out others that present interesting possibilities.

One tool developed specifically for polymer clay is the clay extruder. Similar in appearance and function to a cookie press, this handy device can squeeze out solid logs in a variety of shapes. For best results, make sure your clay is well kneaded and slightly thinned before you start. You can also help soften the clay by running warm water over the extruder for a few minutes. Then extrude the clay shapes using slow, steady pressure to avoid cracking.

To apply textures, assemble an assortment of leaves, fabrics, carved or molded articles, seashells, stones, and other objects. Small paintbrushes are also useful. If you rub just a bit of clay into the bristles, a brush can smooth two surfaces together nicely.

Two types of equipment are needed for baking: one for flat pieces and another for beads. Bake your flat pieces on a nonmetallic surface. A metal surface creates a high gloss on the bottom of your piece and can cause it to singe slightly. If you want to use a cookie sheet, cover it with a piece of oven parchment paper (available at kitchen supply stores) or thin cardboard. Alternatively, use a ceramic tile or plate or a flat piece of unfinished wood. (The low temperatures used should burn neither the cardboard nor the wood.) When you bake beads, they should be suspended so one side doesn't get flattened. Thread several beads onto a piece of wire, and lay several wires across a baking pan. If you have problems with your wires moving, make a tray from cardboard, and cut small slits in each side to hold the wires in place.

OTHER MATERIALS

In conjunction with some of your designs, you may want to add special effects to your polymer clay. Several of the projects in this book (see pages 113, 124, 126, 128, 131, and 140) include metallic leaf, which comes in gold, silver, copper, and various compositions. Available from art supply companies, metallic leaf is sold in booklets containing several small sheets. Each sheet is extremely thin and is easily marked by fingerprints. The effects are worth a bit of extra trouble, however, and you can incorporate whole sheets, cut strips, or small fragments into your designs. When pressed onto the clay with a roller or pasta machine, the leaf will crack, creating some beautiful effects. It is unaffected by baking, but any leaf on the top surface of your jewelry should be coated with varnish to prevent it from discoloring or flaking off.

Eberhard Faber, among others, produces a line of metallic powders that can be brushed onto your pieces before baking. You may also want to experiment with old eye shadow and blush powders. Generally, a little goes a long way, and the powders tend to spread beyond the area you intended to cover. Until you get some experience, it's better to start with a small amount of powder and a very fine brush. For permanence, a powdered surface should also be varnished.

Metallic finishes can also be achieved with wax-based buffing compounds (such as those made by Rub 'n Buff), liquid metallic leaf, or acrylic paints. These are applied after baking, which is an advantage if you want to see and handle the finished piece before deciding if it needs further embellishment.

Additional color and texture can be added to polymer clay with colored markers and pencils, glitters, gemstones, and just about any found objects you can

Materials to embellish your designs include copper and composition leaf, metallic powders, liquid metal leaf, colored pencils, and star-shaped studs.

imagine. Anything that can withstand the baking temperature can be incorporated into a piece before firing. Many smaller items will bond directly to the clay as it bakes, requiring only a light coat of varnish to keep the decorations in place. Larger ones may need to be glued to the clay.

If you don't apply any of the powders or finishes that require a coating of lacquer, you may prefer to leave your finished piece in its natural state. Once baked, polymer clay has a slight sheen to it that is quite attractive. This can be enhanced by buffing the surface with a soft cloth with or without a little paste wax. Both Sculpey and FIMO have complementary varnishes in both gloss and matte finishes, but these must be applied with a brush. If you prefer a spray, you may have to experiment to find a brand you like; not all sprays will dry satisfactorily on polymer clay. Two brands that have been found successful are Duncan Super Matte Ceramic Sealer (a matte finish) and Spray 'n Seal (glossy), a Rub 'n Buff product.

SAFETY

Aside from slicing a finger with a craft knife or single-edged blade, there are few hazards associated with polymer clay. Although it is certified nontoxic, you should always keep your craft tools apart from those you use for food preparation. It is also important to clean your hands thoroughly, removing all traces of clay, before handling food. (Don't snack while you're working without washing first.) Use hand lotion to loosen the clay from your skin; then wipe your hands with paper towels. Baking soda is a gentle, slightly abrasive cleanser that will effectively remove any last remnants of clay.

At its recommended baking temperature, polymer clay creates an interesting, somewhat pleasant aroma. Keep in mind that this is a petroleum-based material and that you shouldn't stand around for prolonged periods of time breathing its fumes. You should also avoid breathing quantities of the dust that is created when you sand or drill a piece of polymer clay that has been fired. Always use good ventilation while baking your clay, and wear a mask if you plan to do any extensive sanding.

The primary hazard that you may encounter with polymer clay results from burning it. If the baking temperature exceeds the manufacturer's recommendation, this material can burn and emit hazardous fumes. The gas produced is acidic and will sting your throat and lungs if you breathe it. Obviously, it will not creep up on you unawares. If burning should occur, do what comes naturally: immediately turn off the oven, open several windows, and vacate the area until the smell has dissipated. Then clean your oven with a suitable detergent.

Unlike the polymer clay, some of the materials you may use with it *are* hazardous. The metallic powders can be very irritating to your throat and lungs if accidentally inhaled. It is strongly recommended that you wear a mask and gloves when applying them. Similarly, liquid metallic leaf products and spray varnishes can also be hazardous if mishandled. Follow the manufacturer's guidelines carefully.

A GALLERY OF DESIGNS

An African-inspired necklace by Susan Kinney.

Right: Fanciful animal pins modelled by Nina Piccirilli.

Below: A large barrette by Steven Ford and David Forlano.

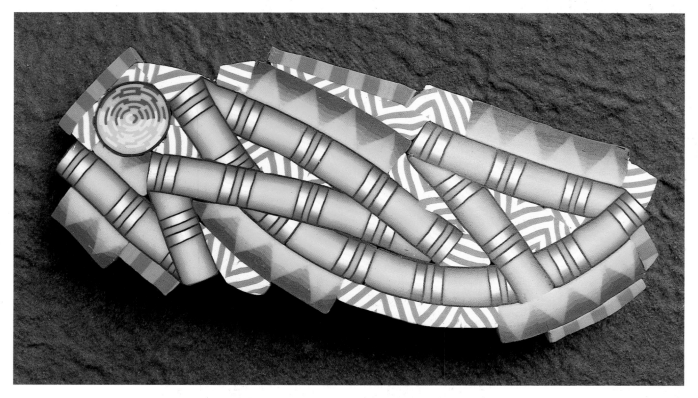

Left: A necklace and earrings in a bumblebee pattern by Nina Piccirilli.

Below: A bumblebee bracelet by Nina Piccirilli.

Right: "Let's Dance,"
a brooch by Claire
Laties Davis.

Below: Alice and
several other
Wonderland
characters decorate
this bracelet by
Kathleen Amt.

Left: A pin "hand woven" by Thessaly Barnett.

Below left: Fish earrings by Nina Piccirilli.

Below: Jester pin and earrings by Bridget Albano.

Opposite: Beauty and function combine in this delightful rosary by Marguerite Kuhl and Jane Vislocky.

JEWELRY-MAKING TECHNIQUES

BASIC SHAPES

Before venturing into the complex designs you can make with polymer clay, practice making a few of the basic forms. These include round balls, flat sheets, and logs of various shapes. Round balls are formed in the palms of both hands by turning and shifting the clay until you have as near-perfect a sphere as you can achieve. After a bit of experience, you'll find that ideal place in your hands and the right amount of pressure you need to create sphere after sphere.

Pierce your round ball to make it into a bead. Holding the ball between the thumb and finger of one hand, gently but firmly push a fine needle into one side. Rotate the needle as you press so that you bore a hole into the clay and don't deform it. When the needle exits the ball on the opposite side, a small bulge of clay may come with it. Smooth this with a finger, and reinsert the needle through the exit hole. If you need to make a large hole to accommodate elastic or leather, make an initial pilot hole with a small needle. Then enlarge the hole with a skewer or other tool.

Making a perfectly uniform flat sheet is a breeze if you have a pasta machine. If you don't, it can be more of a challenge. To flatten a sheet into a thin pancake, start with a ball of clay. Press the ball until it is slightly flattened. Then, using your brayer or rolling pin, roll one or two strokes in each direction. Gently pick up your clay, and turn it over. Roll once or twice more, and turn it again. (The frequent turning helps prevent the clay from sticking to your work surface.) Repeat the process until your clay reaches the thickness you want.

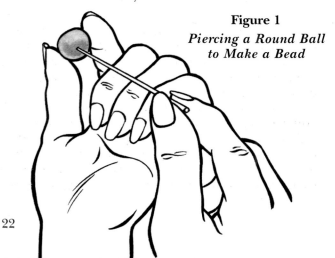

Figure 1
*Piercing a Round Ball
to Make a Bead*

As the sheet gets thinner, you may notice some bubbles under your roller as it comes toward you. Beware of these, and stop rolling as soon as you see them. Pick up the portion of the sheet closest to you, and give it a slight pull before setting it down again. The clay is expanding in surface area as it gets thinner and needs room to grow.

To assure a uniform thickness across your sheet of clay, first cut two dowels whose diameter is equal to the thickness you want your sheet. Place one on either side of your clay, and continue flattening until your roller touches the dowels. This procedure works best if you have a long roller such as a rolling pin or thick dowel. For very thin sheets, you can substitute skewers for the two dowels.

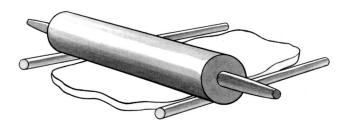

Figure 2
Using Dowels with Your Roller

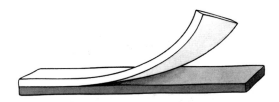

Figure 3
Stacking Sheets of Clay

When you place one sheet on top of another to make layers, always set one end down first. Smoothing two sheets together from one end to another will help avoid trapping air bubbles inside the clay.

Forming a log (or snake) also starts with a round ball. Set it on your work surface, and gently roll it back and forth with the flatter, bottom part of your

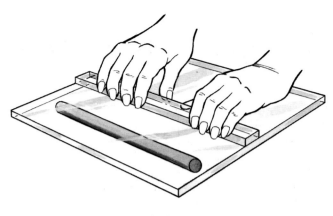

Figure 4
Rolling a Log with a Homemade Plexiglass Tool

hand. Move your hand across the log to avoid making noticeable dents as you roll it, and periodically pick up your log and turn it end for end. When the log becomes too long to handle comfortably, cut it into segments. If you have trouble making a log with a consistent diameter, try using a piece of plexiglass to do your shaping. You can glue a handle to one side of the plexiglass to make it easier to maneuver. Practice rolling logs until you feel comfortable making them in all sizes from less than a millimeter to more than an inch (2.5 cm) in diameter.

Logs are quite useful for making multiple beads. If you cut a log with a uniform diameter into equal-sized segments, you can form each one into an identical round ball. By cutting the segments at different measurements, you can make beads that are graduated in size.

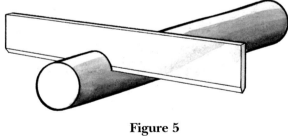

Figure 5
Slicing a Log

To make a good cut without deforming the log, first make sure your blade is clean and sharp and the clay is cool. A heavily worked piece of clay is soft, warm, and easily distorted. If necessary, chill your clay in the refrigerator or freezer for a short period. Then hold your slicing blade perpendicular to the log, and cut straight down gently but firmly. Some

artists like to move the blade back and forth, letting the log roll on the table as they cut it. After each cut, rotate the log a partial turn to further minimize distortion. With practice, you'll soon wield your blade like a pro, cutting everything from long barrels to tissue-thin slices.

Once you get comfortable with making round logs, it's time to try shaping them into squares and triangles. This can be done by pinching and coaxing the clay with your fingers, frequently turning the log to manipulate each side evenly. A brayer is also useful for this purpose. Begin flattening one side with your brayer; then rotate the log, and flatten a second side. Continue flattening and rotating until you have the shape you want.

SIMPLE CANE DESIGNS

All polymer clay designs are created by bonding different colors and shapes of the clay together. Some of the most popular techniques involve making canes, a process originally applied to glasswork. In glassworking, a cane is a glass log with a design running through its entire length. Each slice cut from the cane (like a slice from a jellyroll) shows the pattern. The technique was developed in ancient Egypt, adopted by the Romans, and greatly refined by Venetian glass makers who coined the term *millefiore*, which means thousand flowers, for their delicate, detailed images. Polymer clay artists have adopted the term *millefiore* and often use it interchangeably with "cane" and "loaf" to describe the often complex designs they make.

What do you do with these canes once they're finished? If you cut thick slices, you can make them directly into beads or pendants, piercing them through the edges or through the ends. With several tissue-thin slices, you can decorate a bead or a sheet of clay, assembling complex images from a variety of cane slices. You can even create entire scenes filled with people constructed as canes. They offer an infinite variety of ways to have fun!

The most common example, familiar to all of us, is the candy cane. To make one from polymer clay, roll two logs in contrasting colors. Holding the two logs together at one end, twist the free ends into the characteristic pattern. Try not to twist one log while the other remains straight; this gives a lopsided pattern. An easy way to make sure both logs get twisted evenly is to place them side by side on your work surface, hold one end steady, and pull the other end toward you. You may need to repeat this a few times to get a good twist. Once you have the pattern established, gently roll (but don't twist) the log to smooth its surface.

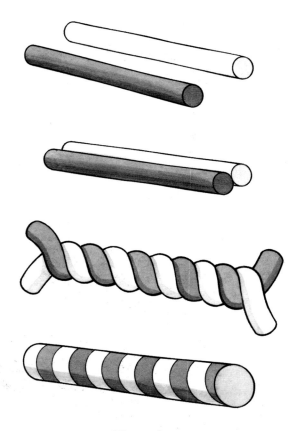

Figure 6
Making a Candy Cane

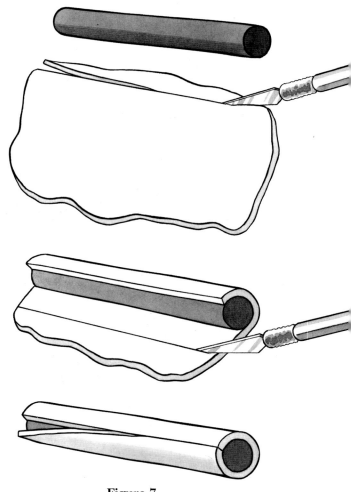

Figure 7
Constructing a Bull's Eye

Another simple pattern is the bull's eye. Start with a log of one color and a sheet of another. The two should be equal in length, and the sheet should be wide enough to wrap more than all the way around the log. Cut a clean, straight edge on one long side of the sheet, and position the log at this edge. Roll the log, wrapping the sheet around it, until the beginning edge of the sheet touches the excess portion. Then open the sheet sufficiently to cut a straight line, making a butt joint where the two edges meet.

The jellyroll is a popular pattern that is not only versatile, it's easy to make. Flatten two or three pieces of clay into long, narrow rectangular sheets, choosing colors that go well together. Lay one on top of another, and lightly flatten one end with your brayer or fingers. Starting at the flattened end, roll the layers into a tight spiral. Gently roll the finished cane to make the seams disappear. You can vary the effects of your jellyroll by staggering the layers, making the bottom ones slightly longer than the top ones, or by adding a solid or multi-colored log in the center.

By stacking two or more sheets of clay, you can make a striped loaf. (Its overall shape is rectangular, resembling a loaf of bread.) Using a simple technique, you can assemble several stripes from just two sheets of clay. Make two thick slabs rectangular in shape, and lay one on top of the other. After trimming the edges to neaten the rectangle, cut the assembly in half.

To cut a rectangular-shaped cane, set the loaf with the shortest side resting on your table. (It's much like cutting a block of cheese.) Holding your blade in both hands, press gently but firmly down through the center of the clay. A little distortion is inevitable, but this can be minimized by using a sharp blade and making sure your clay is cool. For subsequent cuts, turn the loaf so the direction of the distortion changes each time and doesn't become progressively more pronounced.

Figure 8
The Jellyroll

Figure 9
Making a Striped Loaf

After making your cut, place one half on top of the other, maintaining the striped pattern. Then use your roller, or lightly pinch and pull the loaf with your fingers, to lengthen it and make it smaller in diameter. (Strictly speaking, a cane that isn't round doesn't have a "diameter," but to minimize confusion when talking about the size of a cane's cross section, this term is used no matter what overall shape it has.) In the language of cane-making, this is called *reducing* your cane. While the overall length increases, the entire design reduces in size. To keep from distorting the image during this process, turn the cane frequently as you manipulate it. Using this process, you can continue to cut, stack, and reduce your cane until you have a striped loaf with as many layers as you like.

Starting with a large cane and reducing it to a small one is the secret to creating tiny intricate designs your friends won't believe you made by hand. As you decrease the size of your cane, it maintains all of the detail you originally put into it. Your key ingredient is patience. Reduce your canes slowly and evenly, especially the more com-plex ones, and allow them to cool periodically and rest from your manipulations.

In the process of reducing your cane, you'll notice that the ends start to distort dramatically. Don't be alarmed by this; when you cut slices, the perfect design inside will be revealed. Some artists prefer to trim off the distorted parts at each stage of assembly, but this is up to you. If you don't trim off the distorted parts, place them all at the same end when you stack your component pieces. That way, you'll minimize waste.

When you reduce your canes, the ends will distort (see cane at far right), but the image remains true to the original design (see full-size slice in foreground).

Striped loaves come in handy for adding patterns to other logs and other canes. Try this using a log of any color for your center. Cut several thin slices lengthwise from the loaf (or cut slices from the end, and attach them together to make a single sheet as long as your log), and wrap these around the log so the stripes run its full length. The stripes can then be swirled into a barber pole pattern by twisting the cane. Moving your hands in opposite directions, roll one end toward you while you roll the other end away.

Striped loaves can also be used to construct their own patterns. Build a cane with several stripes, and reduce it to the point where you can easily cut it into four segments. After rotating two of the pieces, reassemble the components into a parquet pattern. For more complexity, the parquet can be reduced, cut into four pieces and restacked again.

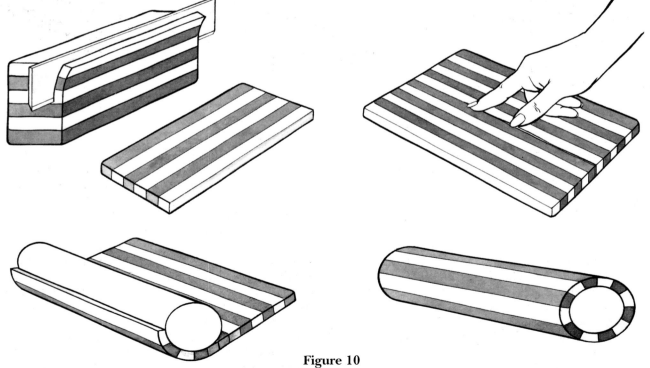

Figure 10

Adding Stripes to a Log or Cane

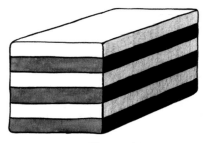

Figure 11
The Parquet Pattern

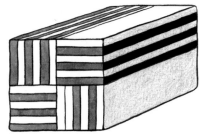

Figure 12
A Complex Parquet

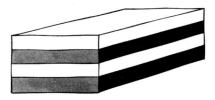

Figure 13
Building a Checkerboard Using a Striped Loaf

One of the most popular design elements is the checkerboard. This can be made by stacking individual square logs in alternating colors, a process made much easier by using a clay extruder. You can also build a checkerboard using a striped loaf. First decide how many squares you want in your checkerboard. Then construct your loaf accordingly. For example, for a four-by-four checkerboard, make your cane four layers high and wide enough to cut four lengthwise slices. The slices should be thick enough to make squares of color when viewed from the ends. After cutting, reverse every other slice, reassemble the loaf into the checkerboard pattern, and compress the elements together tightly.

COMPLEX PATTERNS

Now that you've mastered some of the simpler designs, how about stretching your wings a bit? A complex design isn't necessarily difficult; it's complex because there are several steps involved. A good general rule to remember is to visualize the design in terms of its simple components. Then fit these together as if you were building a three-dimensional mosaic.

To create a flower pattern, the inspiration for the *millefiore*, begin by making a log and cutting it into five segments for petals. You can leave the petals unadorned, but for a bit of added depth, flatten a sheet of clay in a color complementary to that of the petals. Cut the sheet into pieces equal in length to each log segment and wide enough to wrap two-thirds of the way around it. For the flower center, make a log just large enough to fit in the middle so the five petals are touching.

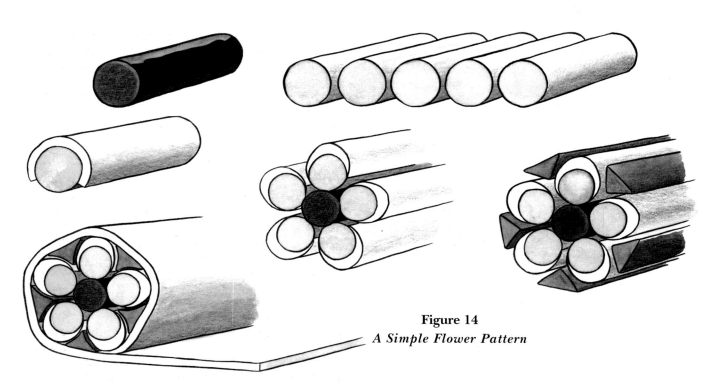

Figure 14
A Simple Flower Pattern

If you stop at this point and roll your cane together, the petals will lose their shape. To maintain the flower intact, you need to fill the empty spaces between the petals with triangular logs of a "background" color. Make a long, triangle-shaped log, and cut it into five pieces, placing one between each pair of petals. Your objective is to fill the cane snugly because wherever there are gaps, the clay will deform to fill them. Once you have all of the components in place, wrap your hands around the cane, and compress it evenly from all sides. To finish the assembly, wrap a sheet of background-colored clay around the cane. You may not want to make a thousand flowers, but you can have as many as you wish by reducing the cane, cutting it into segments and assembling a number of flowers together.

A star is very similar to a flower except that you use triangular canes for points instead of round ones for petals. Form a triangle-shaped log, and cut it into five sections. Then make a round log for the center, and arrange the points evenly around it. As with your flower, make an additional triangular log in a background color and cut it into segments to fit the spaces between the points. Compress all of the pieces together, and finish the assembly with an outer sheath in the background color.

An alternative approach to making a star is to start from the outside. Make a round log in the background color, and slice it lengthwise about

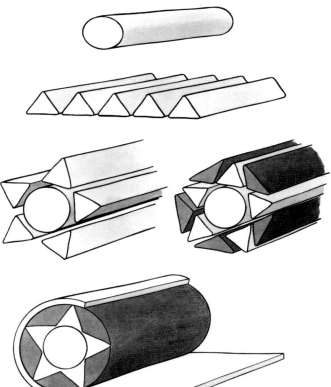

Figure 15
Making a Star

28

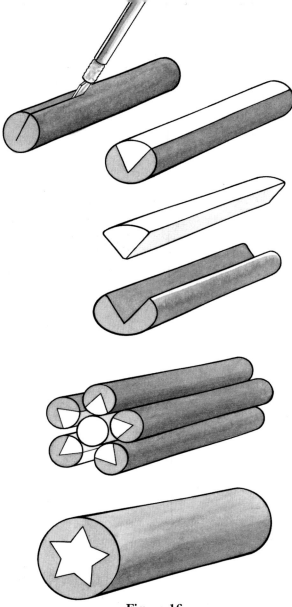

Figure 16
Alternative Method for Making a Star

In general, complex designs require just a bit more patience than do the simpler ones. Although it's difficult to resist the temptation to press ahead, let your cane rest after assembling all of the components. Otherwise, the warmer, softer portions will respond more to your manipulations. For best results, let your cane rest and cool overnight before reducing it or cutting slices.

MAKING A FACE CANE

Some of the most captivating designs created in polymer clay include the human face. Building a face cane is a good bit more complicated than making a flower or star, but if you take your time and work carefully, you'll be thrilled with the results.

When making complex canes, especially faces, it often helps to start with a drawing of the end result you want. Your ideas are bound to change as you work, but the drawing acts as a guide to help you keep the various components in scale with one another. Coloring your drawing and/or dividing the face into areas of color also helps. As you draw, keep the design fairly simple. Canes automatically appear more complex when they are made smaller. Sometimes the meticulous detail apparent at the outset is lost when the cane is reduced to its final size.

Make a colored sketch of the face you plan to construct.

three-quarters of the way through the clay. Now form a triangular log in the color you want for your star. Open the slice in the background log, and lay the triangle inside so the flat edge is exposed, flush with the background. Reduce the cane if necessary, and cut it into five segments. After making another log for the center, arrange the star pieces around it. Make sure the points are even and the triangles are in proper alignment at both ends of your cane. Then compress all of the pieces together, and roll the cane until the seams have disappeared. An outer layer of the background color is optional.

Figure 17

Using the "Paint-by-Number" Approach

Make your drawing about the size you expect your cane to be when you first build it, not the ultimate size you want for your jewelry. Although the clay tends to "grow" as you assemble the cane, a full-size drawing can help you keep the proportions you want. You can actually build your cane on your drawing or place your work right next to it.

The second step is to mix your colors in the shades you want. Be sure to check how they will look when placed close together. Set the shadow color next to the skin color to determine if there is enough contrast between them. Is the cheek color too pink or the eye color too dark?

Using the basic cane-making techniques described above, build the face by assembling the individual components. For example, wrap a black

log with a sheet of blue (or green or brown) for the eye, and place a white triangular log on either side. Make fat circular logs for cheeks. Where you want a strong line defining a feature—perhaps a line along the length of the nose—place a sheet of black clay along one side of the component parts.

There are no hard and fast rules for constructing a face cane; if it works for you, you're doing it right. However, many artists find it helpful to start with the eyes—the "windows to the soul." Placing these together with the nose generally gets your face cane off to a good start.

Continue to fill in the face mosaic-style, shaping the pieces so that you leave as few air pockets as possible. As you can see in the face cane below, the shapes around the cheeks didn't fit well, and the round cheeks deformed. Some distortion is inevitable—and enjoyable—during the process of reducing your cane to its final size. Too much results in an image that is way out of kilter.

After the face is fully constructed, let the cane rest (preferably overnight) to allow all of the components to come to the same temperature. The next step is to compact the cane to remove any gaps. With both hands grasped around your cane, apply even pressure to squeeze the cane together from all sides. Then use your hands to apply downward pressure on both ends of the cane. Repeat both steps until the seams between the sections of clay have disappeared.

Finally, reduce the cane slowly and evenly to the size you want. (You can also cut the cane into sections, reducing each one to a different diameter.) As you would with any cane, apply pressure evenly, and periodically allow the cane to cool and rest. By now the ends of your cane probably look pretty strange, but when you trim off the scrap portion, you'll be amazed and delighted with the results.

Assemble the components of your face cane, compact them together, and reduce the finished image to the diameter(s) you wish. This cane started at 3-1/2 inches (8.9 cm) in diameter and was reduced (at far right) to about 1/2 inch (1.3 cm).

These pieces show two different images made using the same face cane.

SCULPTING A SMALL FACE

An alternative method for including a human face in your jewelry is to model one. Sculpting a human face sounds like a daunting task, but you can make it much simpler by reducing the process to its component elements. Before you begin, assemble the few tools you'll need: one sharp and one very blunt needle tool (a large sewing or darning needle and a blunt tapestry needle, each with a polymer clay handle), one #1 and one #2 paintbrush, and a craft knife. If this is your first experience modelling a face, try making a caricatured face rather than a realistic one. The exaggerated features of a caricature are easier to accomplish. When you're ready to do a more refined face, follow the same steps, but decrease the size of the features, and spend more time blending the lines.

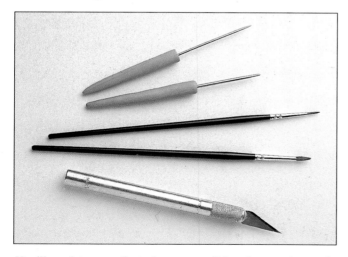

You'll need two needle tools, two small brushes, and a craft knife in order to sculpt a small face.

After thoroughly conditioning your material, roll a smooth ball of clay 3/4 inch (2 cm) in diameter for the head. (To make a smaller or larger face, vary all of the stated dimensions proportionally.) Form the ball into an egg shape, and flatten it slightly. Then, with your blunt needle tool, press a wide mouth shape into the bottom one-third of the egg.

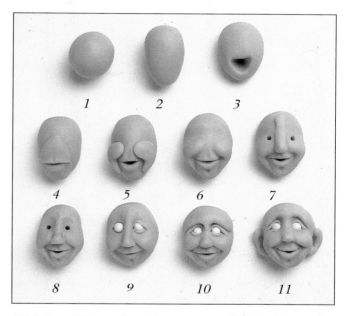

With the addition of each feature, a small ball of clay gradually evolves into a complete human face.

For lips (pieces A and B in the photo on the following page), roll two smooth balls 3/16 inch (5 mm) in diameter. Flatten each ball into a triangular sheet, leaving one edge slightly thicker than the other two. The thicker edge is the actual lip. Make an indentation in the center of the top lip using your blunt needle tool. Place the lip pieces over the mouth opening as shown in face #4 above, using your fingers and blunt tool to blend and smudge the outside edges of the lips into the cheeks and chin.

Roll two balls 1/4 inch (6 mm) in diameter to make the cheeks (C). Then form each into a slightly flattened comma shape. After placing the cheeks around the mouth, roll the blunt needle along the inside cheek lines to blend the mouth and cheeks together. Then blend the outside edges of the cheeks into the face. Any hard-to-reach areas can be smoothed with a paintbrush. Just stroke the bristles lightly with some unbaked clay to stiffen them somewhat.

Make an elongated pyramid shape for the nose using a ball of clay 3/16 inch (5 mm) in diameter.

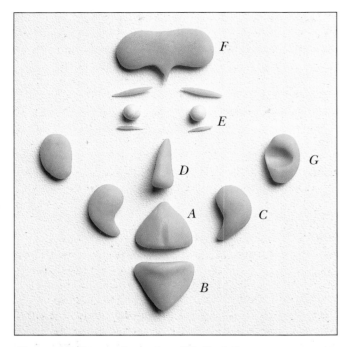

Shape each feature from a small ball of clay.

Set the nose onto the face, depressing it at the bridge, which is just above the middle of the face. Use the blunt needle to shape the nose and blend the edges into the face. Then roll the round, clay end of the tool against the bridge of the nose to form shallow eye sockets.

For simple eyes, make two 1/8-inch (3 mm) balls of white clay, and bake these for ten minutes at 265°F (130°C) for FIMO or 275°F (135°C) degrees for Sculpey III. An iris and pupil can be painted on later. (Otherwise, complete your eyes using slices from a tiny bull's-eye cane.) After they've cooled, press the eyes into the head using the clay end of a needle tool. Mark the corners of the eyes with your sharp needle tool. Then roll tiny commas of clay for eyelids. Position these around the eyes with a sharp needle tool and small paintbrush.

To make the forehead, form a 5/16-inch (8 mm) ball of clay into the shape shown in the photograph (piece F). After flattening it lightly, place the forehead over the eyes. Blend in the edges, taking care not to destroy the eyelids. If desired, use your needle tool to press in some age lines.

Now roll two 1/4-inch (6 mm) balls of clay for the ears. Flatten each slightly into a half-circle, and make a hollow in the center of each ear with the rounded end of your paintbrush handle. Again using the handle of your brush, press the ear onto

the head; then curve the ears slightly forward.

Finish the face by smoothing any remaining rough spots with your brush or needle tools. To add hair, flatten small sheets or ribbons of clay, and press these onto a textured surface, or add hair lines with your sharp needle tool. In addition to hair, you can add hats, hoods, or simply draped fabric. For an example of a finished piece using sculpted faces, see the project on page 116.

MAKING A PRESS MOLD

A third way to make a human face with polymer clay is to mold it. All you need is a small figurine or doll, a soft brush, talcum powder, and some scrap polymer clay. Shape the clay into a pad slightly larger than the face. Then brush some talcum powder lightly onto the doll's face and the pad of clay. Starting in the center and working outward, press the pad down onto the face. Gently remove the pad of clay, and inspect your mold for distortion or missed detail. It may need some gentle reshaping. Then bake the mold using the time and temperature recommended by the polymer clay manufacturer.

When your press mold has cooled, brush the inside lightly with powder. Then, using the clay you want for your face, roll a ball large enough to fill the cavity with some to spare. Elongate one end of the ball into a slight point, and press the clay—pointed end down—into the mold. The pointed end will help ensure you get a complete nose from your mold. Trim off the excess clay that overhangs the mold; then ease the soft clay face out of the mold with your fingers or a wooden modelling tool. If your clay doesn't release well, chill it for about 30 minutes before trying to remove it from the mold. Any irregular edges can be smoothed with your fingers or with a clay-stiffened brush. If desired, use a tapestry needle or other tool to add more definition around the eyes or elsewhere.

OTHER TECHNIQUES

Now that you've had a taste of a few different techniques, you're probably wondering what else this material can do. In the projects that follow, you'll see that you can weave with polymer clay, transfer images onto it, and even "paint" with it. You can draw your own images, add textures and found objects, and model the clay into imaginative shapes and forms. The possibilities for this material are endless. As you explore its range and yours, let your imagination be your guide, and enjoy the process.

STORING YOUR CLAY BETWEEN PROJECTS

Under normal circumstances, unbaked polymer clay doesn't dry out, but long term exposure to direct sunlight can speed aging. It's best to keep your clay covered because it attracts dust, hairs, and other airborne grime. Over time, the oily plasticizer tends to leach out, making a stain if the clay is sitting on a surface such as wood or paper. If left in direct contact with some plastics, polymer clay can actually become bonded. Most clay artists wrap their material in plastic sandwich bags or plastic wrap (some brands are more effective than others) and store it in a cool, dark place.

BAKING

Once you've completed your jewelry pieces and are ready to commit them to the oven, do one last thing first. Look them over carefully for any bits of dirt or other defects. If you notice fingerprints on your work, these can be burnished away. Use a clean, cool, dry finger to swipe lightly and quickly over the print, erasing the telltale ridges. If there are any bubbles, prick them with a fine needle, and smooth the clay flat. After baking, you'll have to resort to sanding, a much more drastic and less desirable solution for correcting such problems.

Always use an oven thermometer to check your oven's temperature during baking.

Figure 18
Making a Press Mold

Whether you use a regular oven or a toaster oven to bake your clay is up to you. Some people feel uncomfortable with the idea of cooking food where they have baked clay, but everything should be fine if you simply air out your oven before popping in your pizza. (After all, this material is nontoxic.) The regular oven offers the advantage of having better temperature control than the toaster models. By all means do NOT try to bake this material in your microwave. It won't explode, but hot spots could occur and cause burning.

Baking times and temperatures recommended by the manufacturers for the most commonly used polymer clays are listed in the table below. You should never exceed these temperatures but you may decide, after gaining some experience, to modify them downward. Many artists regularly use a lower temperature and longer baking time than recommended. With Sculpey and Pro-Mat, underbaking will make your pieces more fragile, but the other brands are not known to suffer when slightly lower temperatures are used. Baking longer than recommended can discolor your clay, especially the lighter colors, but otherwise does no harm. In general, preheat your oven to the recommended temperature, check your temperature during baking with an oven thermometer placed on the shelf where you have your clay, and observe your pieces periodically for undesirable darkening.

Product	Recommended Temperature	Recommended Time
FIMO	265°F (130°C)	20–30 minutes
Sculpey III	275°F (135°C)	10–15 minutes or 15 minutes per 1/4 inch (6 mm) thickness
Pro-Mat	275°F (135°C)	30–45 minutes or 30 minutes per 1/4 inch (6 mm) thickness
Cernit	215–270°F (102–132°C)	5–30 minutes

Most jewelry items are fairly compact, but you should be aware that when polymer clay is first heated, it becomes very soft and can sag. If you have any long, attenuated pieces, brace them with toothpicks or some aluminum foil before placing them in the oven.

In fact, the objects are still somewhat soft when they come out of the oven. Let them cool slowly at room temperature to avoid breaking. Once they're cool, your pieces should be quite hard, and you can test for doneness by tapping them with a fingernail.

One of polymer clay's advantages is its ability to be baked more than once. This is useful if you're making a complex piece and want to include small shapes that may be spoiled if handled while still soft. When returned to the oven, clay that is already baked will bond with the unbaked material.

ASSEMBLING YOUR JEWELRY

Once your polymer clay pieces have been baked and cooled (and varnished, if desired), it takes very little equipment to assemble them into jewelry. For example, if you're making a beaded necklace, the first item you need is a suitable cord for stringing. You want it strong enough to support your beads without breaking but not so heavy that your necklace won't hang gracefully. Carpet or upholstery thread and commercial bead cord made of nylon or Dacron are good alternatives. Beading threads that are waxed may be more resistant than uncoated ones to abrasion from the polymer beads. One of the most popular materials to use is tigertail. Available in thin, medium, and heavy sizes, tigertail is a strong, flexible steel wire coated with plastic. Monofilament (fishing line) is another alternative.

If you use tigertail or monofilament, the material itself is stiff enough to thread your beads. With bead cord or other thread, a beading or darning needle is necessary. Beading needles are handy because they are made to fit through the tiny holes in beads. Many have large eyes—making them easy to thread—that will close slightly when drawn through the bead.

To finish each end of a necklace made with bead cord or thread, use a bead tip. Available in gold and silver, a bead tip is essentially a half-sphere with an attached hook. Thread one onto your cord after the last bead, facing the hook away from the bead. Tie a double knot, and tighten it into the cup of the bead tip. Then secure the knot with a little glue, trim off the excess cord, and close the hook through the end of your clasp.

Use crimp beads to finish the ends of tigertail or monofilament, neither of which can hold a secure knot. After your last polymer bead, thread a crimp bead onto your strand. Then thread the tigertail through one end of your clasp and back through the crimp bead in the opposite direction. Pull the strand so that the crimp and clasp are close together, and tighten the crimp with needle-nose pliers or a crimping tool.

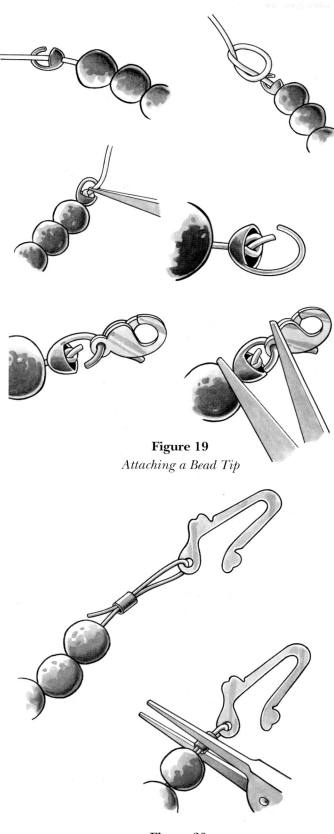

Figure 19
Attaching a Bead Tip

Figure 20
Finishing Tigertail with a Crimp

Necklace clasps can be purchased in many shapes and sizes, or they can be made by hand.

Clasps come in many shapes and sizes, and you can even fashion your own from wire. Another method of closure is to make a button-and-loop clasp. A polymer clay bead is your button, and the loop can be made from knotted thread or twisted wire.

Other findings that you may need include pin backs, barrette clips, and a variety of items for making earrings: ear wires, posts, ear clips, and screw backs. A head pin—an enlarged version of a straight pin—is used to make the dangles for your earrings. Assemble your beads onto the pin, and clip off the excess, leaving about 3/8 inch (1 cm) to close into a loop. Eye pins are similar to head pins but have a loop at one end instead of a flat head.

To open and close findings and to shape wire for your jewelry, two types of pliers are recommended: one pair of needle-nose or chain-nose pliers and one pair of round-nose pliers. The needle-nose pliers from your workshop have grooves on the inside surfaces and will mar your jewelry (although you can cover the grooves with tape in a crunch). The ones intended for jewelry making are better; they have smooth jaws that won't leave marks. The small round-nose pliers are good for bending round wire without leaving any crease marks.

Other handy tools include crimp forming pliers, a sharp pair of wire cutters, and a small jewelry file. The crimping tool enables you to close a crimp so that it resembles a bead instead of mashing it flat.

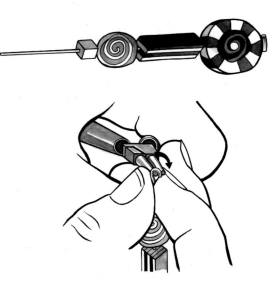
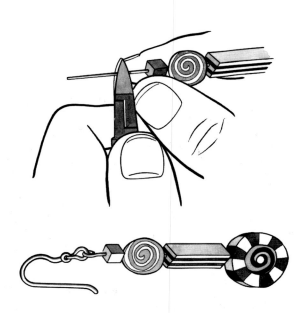

Figure 21
Shaping a Head Pin for an Earring

When choosing a pair of wire cutters, keep in mind that side cutters are more versatile than end cutters. The pointed ends of the side cutters make them much easier to maneuver into tight areas. For a good file to smooth the sharp ends of your freshly cut wire, seek out an auto parts store. The files used for cleaning distributor points are perfect for jewelry-making purposes.

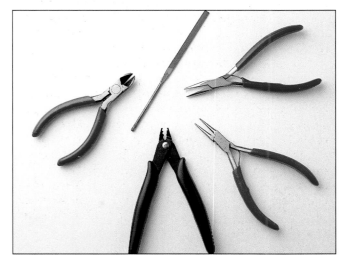

Some tools that are helpful for assembling your jewelry include (clockwise starting at the top): chain-nose pliers, round-nose pliers, a crimping tool, cutters, and a small file.

Findings such as pin backs can be glued to polymer clay with a variety of adhesives. Sculpey's manufacturer recommends using a flexible, styrene-based glue such as E-6000. Quicker to harden are the two-part epoxy cements (recommended by Eberhard Faber) and the cyanoacrylate ("super") glues. Hot-melt glue guns can also be used, but the bond will not be very strong. Water-based glues are not satisfactory for use with polymer clay. Experiment with scraps of baked clay and some extra findings until you find the adhesive that works best for you.

Before applying any glue, remove the oily residue that is present on findings such as pin backs and ear posts. A quick swipe with a cotton ball dampened with rubbing alcohol works well. Otherwise, your findings may not adhere properly to the clay.

HANDLING THE FINISHED PRODUCT

Once baked, polymer clay is generally quite sturdy, and the colors will not fade. However, it's not recommended that you store your jewelry on your windowsill where it will be exposed to hot sunlight day after day. If treated with care, polymer clay buttons can be laundered in cool water and air dried. Don't put your articles in the dryer; the heat is probably not sufficient to harm them, but they may be damaged by hitting the sides of the machine. Dry cleaning is also not recommended.

A FEW WORDS ABOUT THE PROJECTS

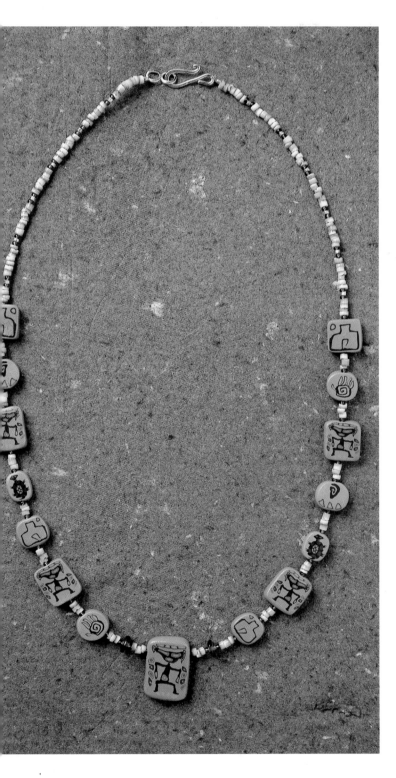

Each of the artists who contributed designs for this book has an individual style. That style is reflected in both the approach to the material and the results obtained; it best serves as a point of departure for your own creativity. Don't be disappointed if your canes look different from those you see here and, by all means, don't feel constrained by the shapes, patterns, brands, or colors chosen by the artists. Polymer clay is a compelling medium, one that encourages experimentation and discovery. Feel free to make substitutions in the materials (brands and/or colors) and to alter the designs. Let these projects be the starting point for your own unique creations.

By way of a caveat, keep in mind that the quantity of materials specified for each project is approximate. While some artists enjoy working on a small scale, others prefer to make each cane quite large before reducing it to the finished size. Some projects call for a large amount of clay simply because several complex canes are used in the final design. Since you're likely to use only portions of the canes for one piece of jewelry, you'll have plenty left over to use for other projects later.

The baking times and temperatures are those actually used by the artists who originated the projects. The different combinations reflect their experiences with their baking equipment. Until you feel comfortable setting your own guidelines, it is strongly recommended that you use the standards set by the manufacturers.

You'll also notice that these projects vary considerably in their level of complexity. Remember, complexity doesn't necessarily make some more difficult than others, just more time consuming. They also vary somewhat in the level of detail provided for you to complete the design. If you've never worked with polymer clay before, select those that specify exactly how each pattern is created. Once you feel more adventuresome, try some of the more abstract and free-form designs. Above all, relax and enjoy the material; let it take you where it may.

Inspired by ancient Mexican designs, this "dancing man" necklace was crafted by Irene Dean.

STRIPES AND SWIRLS

Marbleized Wafer Beads

Materials

*scraps of several colors of
   Sculpey III totaling about
   2 blocks*
*31 - 4 mm round silver
   beads*
tigertail jewelry wire
2 crimp beads
clasp

Tools

slicing blade
piercing tool
*needle-nose pliers or
   crimping tool*

Instructions

1. Begin with small pieces of clay in a rainbow of
   colors. Gather these into a ball, and form a large
   log. To achieve the marbled effect, twist the log
   along its length, and continue manipulating the
   clay until you have a blend you like.

2. Using your slicing blade, cut the log into 30
   even increments to create beads of a consistent
   size. Use the palms of your hands to shape each
   piece into a ball; then flatten it into a thick,
   round wafer.

3. Pierce all of the beads through their edges,
   and bake them at 275°F (135°C) for about
   15 minutes.

4. Alternating the polymer and silver beads, string
   all of the beads onto tigertail. Finish the ends
   with crimp beads, and attach the clasp.

Swirling Stripes

Materials

*1/4 block light turquoise
  FIMO*
1/4 block black FIMO
*1/4 block golden yellow
  FIMO*
38 - #6/0 black glass beads
*16 gold-plated "hogan"
  beads (rondelles)*
tigertail jewelry wire
2 crimp beads
clasp

Tools

*slicing blade
piercing tool
needle-nose pliers or
  crimping tool*

Instructions

1. Roll each color of clay into a thin log about 4 inches (10.2 cm) long. Then stack the three colors, and roll them gently together. Holding one end of the triple log, roll the other end toward you. To achieve a tight spiral design, you may need to twist the log quite a bit. Roll the cane to smooth the outer surface and reduce it somewhat.

2. After the cane has cooled and rested, cut 12 or 14 beads about 3/4 inch (1.9 cm) in length. Pierce each one through the ends.

3. The center bead is a larger chunk of the log that is first rolled on a flat work surface then modelled into a somewhat oval shape using both hands. Pierce this bead through the sides near the top.

4. With your oven set at 265°F (130°C), bake all of the beads for about 40 minutes.

5. Using tigertail to string your necklace, insert two glass beads and one gold-plated hogan as spacers between the polymer beads. Finish the ends with crimps and a clasp.

Classic Stripes

Materials

1/4 block violet FIMO
1/4 block lilac FIMO
1/4 block light turquoise FIMO
1/4 block white FIMO
enough scrap clay to make 25 beads (see below)
30 - #6/0 dusty purple beads
50 - #11/0 pearl beads
tigertail jewelry wire
2 crimp beads
clasp

Tools

rolling tool
slicing blade
piercing tool
needle-nose pliers or crimping tool

Instructions

1. Flatten the three colored clays into rectangular sheets about 1/8 inch (3 mm) thick and twice as long as they are wide. Cut the white clay into thirds, and flatten each section into a thinner sheet equal in size to the first ones.

2. Stack the layers as follows: violet, white, lilac, white, light turquoise, white. After compressing the stack gently, cut it in half crosswise. Then place one half on top of the other.

3. Using a roller or your fingers, compress each side to reduce and lengthen the cane until it measures about 3/8 inch (1 cm) wide and 1-1/4 inch (3.2 cm) high.

4. When the cane is sufficiently reduced, cut four slices about 1/16 inch (about 1.6 mm) thick, and lay them on a smooth surface, one next to another, lining up the stripes.

5. Take a piece of scrap clay about the size of a marble, and roll a log that is equal in length to the four sheets together. Then wrap the log with the sheets, rolling it gently to blend the seams. Continue rolling until the log is about 2-1/2 to 3 inches (about 6 to 8 cm) long.

6. Now slice the covered log into four equal-sized beads. Smooth all of the edges, and pierce the beads through the ends.

7. Repeat the process to make a total of at least twenty beads. For added interest, two or more of your smaller ones can be rolled into round beads. Be sure to make one slightly longer and thicker to place in the center.

8. Bake all of the beads at 265°F (130°C) for about 40 minutes.

9. Before actually stringing your beads, it pays to arrange them in order. Place the largest in the center, and gradually decrease the size toward the ends. When threading the beads onto the tigertail, use a combination of two pearl beads and one dusty purple glass bead as spacers between the polymer clay beads.

10. To finish, just crimp the ends, and attach your clasp.

Bull's Eyes Galore

Materials

1/4 block lavender FIMO
1/8 block yellow FIMO
1/4 block forest green FIMO
enough scrap clay to make
    25 beads (see below)
gloss (optional)
1 mm waxed cotton cord
26 - 6 mm gold-plated beads
fine-gauge jewelry wire or
    two head pins

Tools

rolling tool
slicing blade
piercing tool (skewer
    or other larger tool)
needle-nose pliers

Instructions

1. For this design, start with a simple bull's-eye cane (see page 24 for details). Roll the lavender clay into a log, and flatten the yellow clay into a thin sheet large enough to wrap completely around the log. Trim the sheet, making a butt joint around the log. Now flatten the green clay into a somewhat thicker sheet large enough to fit completely around the log. Then wrap the green sheet around the log, cutting off any excess to give a clean butt joint. Smooth the seams by gently rolling the cane.

2. Continue rolling, reducing the cane, until it is about 4 inches (10.2 cm) long. Then cut the log in half, and roll the two halves together to make a simple cane.

3. Once the cane looks symmetrical, cut it into five equal segments. Stack the parts, and roll them together once again.

4. Finally, cut the cane into thirds. After rolling the parts together to blend the seams, reduce the completed cane until it is 3/8 to 5/8 inch (1 to 1.6 cm) in diameter.

5. While your cane is resting and cooling, use your scrap clay to make 25 round beads. Start with beads about 3/8 inch (1 cm) in diameter, gradually increasing to a single bead about 3/4 inch (1.9 cm) in diameter. For the closure, make an additional bead in a flattened oval shape.

6. Using a sharp blade, cut very thin slices from your cane, and apply them to your beads. Don't worry if the edges overlap; these won't be noticeable in the finished necklace. Cover each bead completely.

7. Pierce the round beads through the center with a skewer or other tool large enough to make a hole that will accommodate the cotton cord. Place two holes in the closure bead. Then bake all the beads at 265°F (130°C) for approximately 40 minutes.

8. After they've cooled, string the beads on the cord, placing the largest bead in the center and the smallest at each end. Each clay bead is separated by a 6 mm gold-plated bead.

9. To attach the closure bead, run the cord up through one hole and back down through the other. Then make a corresponding loop at the other end of the necklace. Use a piece of fine-gauge jewelry wire or a head pin to wrap the cord tightly to itself to secure both ends. Pliers will help you get the wrapping tight.

Jellyroll High Jinks

Materials

1/8 block golden yellow FIMO
1/8 block lilac FIMO
1/8 block light blue FIMO
1 block black FIMO
tigertail jewelry wire
32 - 6/0 black beads
52 - 8/0 dusty purple beads
2 crimp beads
blue telephone wire
2 head pins
2 French hooks

Tools

rolling tool
slicing blade
piercing tool
needle-nose pliers or crimping tool

Instructions

1. To make the jellyroll that is the basis for this design, flatten the golden yellow clay into a sheet twice as long as it is wide and about 1/16 inch (1.6 mm) thick. Trim off the edges to make a neat rectangle. Using black clay, make a second sheet as wide as the first but about 3/8 inch (1 cm) longer and about half as thick. Then center the yellow sheet on top of the black, allowing the black to overextend slightly on each end. Using your fingers or a roller, flatten one end into a wedge. Gently but firmly, roll from the flattened end until you have a jellyroll. Smooth the cane, and continue rolling it until it reaches a length of about 2-1/2 inches (6.4 cm).

2. Repeat the above steps, using lilac rolled in black, and light blue rolled in black. All three canes should have approximately the same length and diameter. If not, roll them to equal diameters, and cut off any excess length.

3. Stack the three jellyrolls, and gently roll them together. Continue rolling until the seams disappear and the cane reaches approximately 6 inches (15.2 cm) in length.

4. Now cut this cane into thirds, stack the pieces, and roll them together to make the final cane pattern. Then reduce the cane to about 3/8 inch (1 cm) in diameter.

5. While your cane is resting, make 22 balls, each about 3/8 inch (1 cm) in diameter, using black clay. To make them all a uniform size, cut equal segments from a log 3/8 inch (1 cm) in diameter. In addition, make six more base beads from black clay: one measuring 1/4 inch (6 mm),

four 5/8 inch (1.6 cm), and one 3/4 inch (1.9 cm) in diameter. The smallest bead is used for a button-and-loop closure; two of the 5/8-inch (1.6 cm) beads are made into earrings; the others become the central beads in the necklace.

6. Using very thin slices cut from your cane, cover all of the beads with the cane pattern. Edges of the pattern slices may overlap, or you may need to patch an empty space with a half slice. Then form two of the 5/8-inch (1.6 cm) beads into barrel shapes to use for earrings.

7. Pierce all of the beads, and bake them at 275°F (135°C) for approximately 40 minutes.

8. Despite your efforts to make all of your beads uniform in size, some will be larger than others. Before stringing them, arrange your beads so the largest is in the center, and the rest diminish in size toward the ends. Add three black beads; then string the clay beads, separating each with a black bead sandwiched between two purple ones. End with three black spacers. Then form a loop of coiled telephone wire, and finish with a crimp bead to secure the loop.

9. To make the earrings, thread the barrel-shaped beads and a trio of spacers onto the head pins. Snip off any excess wire, and form a loop to attach to the French hook. For an added touch, replace the ball and coil on the hooks with a purple bead and a coil of purple niobium.

Checkerboard Chic

Materials

1 block black Sculpey III
2 blocks white Sculpey III
1-1/2 blocks green Sculpey III
1/2 block red Sculpey III
1/2 block yellow Sculpey III
1/2 block orange Sculpey III
2 blocks blue Sculpey III
2-1/2 blocks purple brilliant Sculpey III
tigertail jewelry wire
52 - 3 mm silver beads
48 - 5 mm midnight blue glass beads
2 crimp beads
silver clasp
2 silver head pins
2 ear wires

Tools

rolling tool
slicing blade
piercing tool
needle-nose pliers or crimping tool

Instructions

1. Begin by mixing the colors you want to use for the complex cane. In this necklace, the yellow and orange have been blended and lightened with small amounts of white. To make a light blue, start with a little white clay, and gradually add blue until you have a shade you like.

2. For the center element of the cane, build a four-by-four black and white checkerboard. One method is to stack 16 individual logs. Alternatively, make a striped loaf using two layers of black and two of white. Cut four lengthwise slices, and reassemble the cane with every other slice reversed to make the checkerboard. (See page 27 for more details.)

3. Next, flatten some green clay into a sheet, and trim it to fit completely around the checkerboard cane. Make sure the edges butt together and don't overlap.

4. Using less than a block of each color, build two simple striped loaves: one using four layers of blue and three of light blue, and the other with four layers of green and three of purple. Then reduce the loaves until you can cut each one into three segments. Each segment should be about the same length as the checkerboard cane but much smaller in diameter.

5. Now make a purple and blue jellyroll (see pages 24–25). Reduce it, and cut it into four equal parts, all about the same length as the other components.

6. Roll solid logs in red, light orange, and yellow in various diameters, all smaller than the striped and jellyroll canes. Make each one long enough to cut into five or six segments. Now let all of the components cool to the same temperature.

7. With all of your components ready, assemble the complex cane by placing the checkerboard in the center and surrounding it with a random assortment of the solid, striped, and jellyroll canes. Alternate the solid and patterned canes, trying not to cluster multiples of the same cane in one area.

8. Gently roll all the elements together, and reduce the complex cane until it is about 1/2 inch (1.3 cm) in diameter. After the cane has rested and cooled, slice it into 22 disk-shaped beads about 1/8 inch (3 mm) thick.

9. Make the purple spacers by rolling a solid purple log about 3/8 inch (1 cm) in diameter and slicing it into 46 disks, each about 1/8 inch (3 mm) thick.

10. Pierce all of the solid purple beads through the center of the flat sides, and the patterned beads through the edges. Bake them all at 275°F (135°C) for about 15 minutes.

11. After the beads have cooled, assemble them onto the tigertail. The pattern is a seven bead repeat after the initial silver bead: one blue, one silver, two solid purple disks, one silver, one blue, and one patterned disk. Finish at the opposite end with another silver bead.

12. Crimp the ends of the tigertail, and add your clasp.

13. For each earring, assemble a pattern sequence of beads onto a head pin. Twist the top of the pin into a loop, and attach it to the ear wire.

Jellyrolls à la Mode

Materials

1 block yellow FIMO
2 blocks green FIMO
1 block black FIMO
1 block white FIMO
1/2 block blue FIMO
1-1/2 blocks red FIMO
48 - #6/0 glass beads in
   bottle green or black
tigertail jewelry wire
2 crimp beads
2 head pins
2 ear wires

Tools

rolling tool
slicing blade
piercing tool
needle-nose pliers or
   crimping tool

Instructions

1. Begin by flattening 1/2 block each of yellow and green clay into long rectangular sheets. Placing the yellow on top of the green, roll these into a jellyroll. (See pages 24–25 for more details on making jellyrolls.)

2. Using about 1/4 block each of black and white clay, flatten both into thin sheets large enough to wrap around the jellyroll. Apply the black first, followed by white. Then reduce the cane until you can cut it into four equal segments each about 3 inches (about 7.5 cm) long.

3. Recombine the four segments into a single complex cane, and roll the cane gently until it is smooth and the seams disappear.

4. Roll the remaining black and white clay into logs about 3/16 inch (about 5 mm) in diameter. Cut both logs into 16 or 17 segments, each as long as your cane. Alternating black and white segments, position the logs around the cane so it appears the cane has lengthwise stripes. (See Figure 1.) It should take about six logs of each color to cover the outside of the cane. Using the rest of the logs, alternate black and white to make a second layer. Place black on top of white to give a somewhat checkered appearance to the cross section. Then roll the cane until it is smooth.

5. Finally, wrap the cane in a sheet of blue, then one of yellow, then green, then red. Wrap each layer so that the edges butt together (as you would a bull's-eye cane, see page 24). Then trim the ends, and reduce the cane until it is about 3/8 inch (1 cm) in diameter. This completes your primary cane pattern.

6. Using your trimmings or other scrap clay, make one or more logs about 3/8 inch (1 cm) in diameter to use for your base beads. To make four medium-sized cylinder beads, cut a segment about 4-1/2 inches (about 11.5 cm) long, and cover it with paper-thin slices of the cane, overlapping the slices to completely cover the base color. After rolling and smoothing the slices onto the log, cut it into four beads, each about 7/8 inch (about 2 cm) long. Pierce each one lengthwise.

7. Now cut ten segments from your log made of scrap material. Make each segment 3/8 inch (1 cm) long, and roll these into balls. Using thin slices from the cane, cover the round beads entirely. Then pierce each one.

8. For slightly larger round beads, cut eight 1/2-inch (1.3 cm) segments from the base log. Roll these into balls, cover them with cane slices, and pierce.

9. To make the barrel beads, cut a segment of the base log about 8 inches (about 20 cm) long. After covering it entirely with cane slices, roll and smooth the covered log. Then cut six segments 1 inch (2.5 cm) long, and coax them into

Figure 1

barrel shapes by lightly squeezing the ends of each segment. Pierce each one lengthwise.

10. For the "eye" beads (flattened barrel shapes), cut a segment of the base log about 4 inches (10 cm) long. Cover it entirely with cane slices, and cut three pieces about 7/8 inch (2.2 cm) long. Form these into barrels, pierce, and gently flatten them into the "eye" shape.

11. To make the complementary striped pattern, flatten one block each of red and green clay into thin sheets about 2 inches (about 5 cm) wide by 15 inches (about 39 cm) long. Lay one on top of the other, and cut the assembly into 15 short sections. Stack the pieces to form a striped cane.

12. With the remaining scrap clay, roll two 1/2-inch (1.3 cm) balls, one log 1/2 inch (1.3 cm) in diameter and 4 inches (about 10 cm) long, and one log 1/4 inch (6 mm) in diameter and 3 inches (about 7.5 cm) long. Cover all four with thin slices from the striped cane. Then reduce the two logs slightly, and cut each into four segments. With two of the larger log segments, pinch the ends to form barrel shapes. Then pierce all of the striped beads.

13. Bake all of the beads at 250°F (120°C) for about 30 minutes.

14. After they've cooled, string the beads onto the tigertail as shown in the photo, reserving two barrels and two smaller round beads for the earrings. Remember to place one glass bead between each polymer bead and at each end of the string.

15. To make the endless circle (without a clasp), string two crimp beads onto one end of the tigertail. Then insert that end of tigertail through the glass bead on the other end of the necklace, and into the polymer bead next to it. Grasp the end of the tigertail with your pliers as it comes through the clay bead, and gently pull until the beads are all fairly close together. Now take the other end of the tigertail and insert it through the crimps (in the opposite direction), through the glass bead, and through the first polymer bead. Grasp that end with the pliers, and pull gently but firmly until all of the beads are snug. Keeping the ends of the tigertail taut, flatten the crimps.

16. For the earrings, thread the clay and glass beads onto the head pins as shown in the photo. Form a loop at the end of each head pin, and attach the dangles to the ear wires.

"Double Link" Quilt Pattern

Materials

3 blocks black Sculpey III
3 blocks white Sculpey III
enough scrap clay to make 29 beads (see below)
30 - 6 mm black rondelles
59 - 3 mm silver beads
tigertail jewelry wire
2 crimp beads
clasp

Tools

clay extruder (recommended) or rolling tool
slicing blade
piercing tool
needle-nose pliers or crimping tool

Instructions

1. Begin with equal amounts of two contrasting colors and about four times as much of the background color. This piece uses a classic black, white, and gray combination. To create the gray used here, add one part black clay to one part white, and mix well.

2. The pattern consists of a total of 100 individual square logs arranged according to the grid in Figure 1. A clay extruder makes this job easier and may keep you from crying "uncle." Alternatively, you can flatten some clay into a slab, and cut individual strips that are as wide as they are thick. Whichever method you choose, assemble the components and compress them together using even pressure with both hands. Maintain the overall square shape, using a roller to flatten the sides.

3. Once the initial cane is to your liking, cut it into four segments and reassemble the pieces into a square-shaped loaf. Then reduce this complex cane until it is approximately 1/2 inch (1.3 cm) in diameter.

4. While your cane is resting, form 29 cube-shaped base beads from leftover clay, each equal in diameter to your cane. (With this pattern, it is easier to begin with cubes and later round them into spheres.)

5. Apply one thin slice of the cane to each of the six sides of each cube. When you have finished all 29, round them into balls.

6. Pierce all of the beads, and bake them at 275°F (135°C) for about 15 minutes.

7. Assemble the polymer beads onto the tigertail, separating each one with a trio of spacer beads: two silver and one black rondelle. Finish with crimp beads and the clasp of your choice.

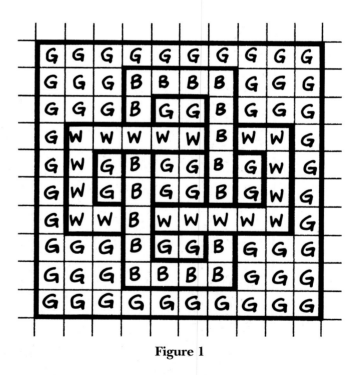

Figure 1

Leapin' Lizards!

Materials

4 blocks white FIMO
1 block black FIMO
3 blocks green or turquoise
   FIMO
enough scrap clay to make
   19 beads (see below)
18 - 6 mm marble beads
6 - 4 mm hematite beads
8 - 10 mm howlite beads
8 - 6 mm turquoise beads
2 - 4 x 13 mm rectangular
   turquoise beads
6 - 4 mm square hematite beads
14 black seed beads
silver rondelle spacers
heavy nylon thread
2 bead tips
clasp

Tools

rolling tool
slicing blade
piercing tool
beading or darning needle

Instructions

1. Start by making a black and white jellyroll (see
   pages 24–25 for details on making jellyrolls). You'll
   need only a minimal amount of material—less than
   1/4 block of each color—to make a jellyroll of sufficient size for this necklace. (Any excess can always
   be used for another project.) Then reduce the
   cane to about 1/8 inch (3 mm) in diameter.

2. Using about 1/4 block of each color, make a
   second small cane of black and white polka dots.
   Each dot is simply a black and white bull's eye
   (see page 24). Reduce the bull's eye, and cut it
   into many dots as you want for your cane.
   This one includes one central dot surrounded
   by five others. If the dots deform when you
   reduce the cane, don't worry; the pattern is
   meant to be abstract.

3. Now make a small green and white jellyroll
   cane, again using about 1/4 block of each color.
   Then surround the jellyroll with four small logs
   of black and four of white, alternating the two
   colors. After reducing this cane until you can
   cut it into six equal segments, arrange the pieces
   so you have one in the center, surrounded by
   five others. Roll the finished cane to smooth the
   seams, but don't reduce it beyond about 3/4
   inch (1.9 cm) in diameter.

4. The lizard is a complex cane, and you should
   make it whatever size feels most comfortable to
   you. (Remember, large-diameter canes can be
   quite short; when reduced, they lengthen sub-
   stantially.) Depending on how large you make
   the cane, you may have more than enough
   material remaining, or you may need to add
   some. Start your cane with the head. Make two
   eyes—black and white bull's-eye canes—and
   cover each with a sheet of green clay. Build a
   teardrop-shaped head by wedging small green
   triangles between the eyes and a larger green
   triangle on top (Figure 1). Wrap all of the

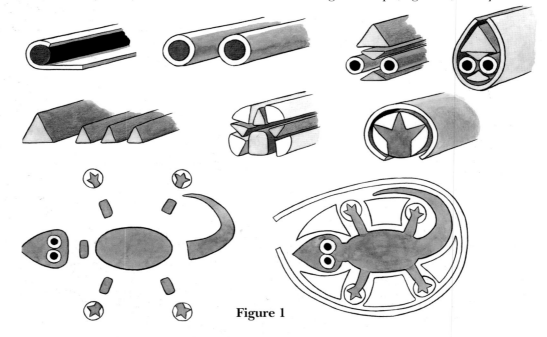

Figure 1

components in a sheet of green clay.

5. Next construct the feet. The toes are simplified into triangles, and each foot is a rounded square log. After assembling the green components, make wedge-shaped logs of white clay to fill the areas between the toes and on either side of the foot. Finally, wrap a sheet of white clay around the foot, making sure to exclude the portion that will attach to the leg (refer to Figure 1).

6. Now make an oval log for the body and rounded rectangles for the legs and neck. After making a thick slab for the tail, flatten one side with your roller and curve it to look more "taillike." Join all of the body parts together, and use white logs in various shapes and sizes to fill in the gaps and make an overall oval-shaped cane. Once you've wrapped everything together with a sheet of white clay, voilà, you've created a lizard. Reduce him to about 5/8 inch (1.6 cm) in diameter.

7. Using your scrap clay, form one base bead about 3/4 inch (about 2 cm), 16 beads 1/2 inch (1.3 cm), and two beads 1/4 inch (6 mm) in diameter.

8. Having finished all of the components, now you're ready to assemble your beads. Cut thin slices from the lizard cane, and apply them to the largest base bead and to two of the mid-size beads. After the designs are in place, shape the mid-size beads into cubes. Then cut two slices 1/4 inch (6 mm) thick from the complex green jellyroll to use as disk beads. Cover two of the mid-size base beads with thin slices of the green jellyroll (you may need to reduce it somewhat), and cover two more with slices from the black and white jellyroll. Now apply slices of the polka-dot cane to eight of the mid-size beads, and shape two of them into cubes. The remaining two mid-size beads in this necklace are covered with black and white stripes twisted at one end into a swirl. For simplicity, substitute slices from one of the three canes you've already made. For the two smallest beads, you'll need to reduce the lizard until he is a miniature, only a few millimeters long. Then cut thin slices to cover the two beads.

9. Pierce all of the beads, including the two thick slices, and bake them at 250°F (120°C) for about 30 minutes.

10. Using two strands of heavy nylon, string the polymer beads and stone beads as shown in the photo. Finish the ends with bead tips and a clasp.

Abundance of Riches

Materials

2 blocks yellow FIMO
3 blocks violet FIMO
3 blocks carmine FIMO
3 blocks light turquoise FIMO
2 blocks orange FIMO
2 blocks mother-of-pearl FIMO
1/2 block pink FIMO
2 bead tips
heavy nylon thread
clasp

Tools

rolling tool
ruler
slicing blade
piercing tool
beading or darning needle

Instructions

1. Making an embellished jellyroll—one with a solid-colored center and stripes around the outside—is the first step for this necklace. Begin by flattening 1/4 block of light turquoise and 1/4 block of pink clay into long, narrow rectangular sheets and rolling about 1/8 block of carmine clay into a log. Place the light turquoise sheet on top of the pink and, with the carmine log on one end, roll the sheets around the log into a jellyroll. (See Figure 1.)

2. Now make the first of two striped loaves (see pages 24–25 for details). Using 1/4 block of carmine and 1/4 block of yellow, assemble the loaf with two layers of each color. After cutting the loaf in half, flatten 1/4 block of violet clay into a slab the same length and width as one of the loaf segments. Stack the loaf pieces, placing the violet slab in the center, so the same color stripe is on the outside top and bottom.

3. Make a second striped loaf using one layer of pink and one of violet (1/4 block of each color). Cut the loaf in half, and reassemble it with a center stripe made from 1/4 block of light turquoise.

4. After cutting three or four lengthwise slices from each striped loaf, wrap the slices around the jellyroll—alternating the colors—so the stripes run lengthwise. (See page 26 for details on adding stripes to canes.) Reserve the balance of the striped loaves for use later. Then gently roll the cane, and reduce it to about 1/2 inch (1.3 cm) in diameter.

5. Make a second, simple jellyroll (see pages 24–25) using 1/4 block of carmine and 1/4 block of

light turquoise clay. Reduce this cane to a diameter of about 1/2 inch (1.3 cm).

6. To make the flower cane, form a log for the petals from 1/4 block of light turquoise clay, cut it into five equal segments, and wrap a sheet of yellow clay about two-thirds around each piece. (See pages 27–28 for more details.) Place these around a central violet log, making sure all the petals touch and the yellow sheets face outward. Using 1/4 block of carmine clay, shape five triangles to wedge between the petals and round out the cane, and use an equal amount of carmine to cover the cane with an outer sheath. When complete, reduce the cane to about 1/2 inch (1.3 cm) in diameter.

7. Next make a star cane using approximately 1/4 block of orange clay for the points. Roll the clay into a triangular-shaped log, and cut it into five equal sections. From the complex (first) jellyroll, cut a short segment to use for the center element of the star. Arrange the orange points around the central jellyroll, making sure the bottom edges of the triangles all touch. (See Figure 2.) You may need to reduce the jellyroll to get a proper fit. Using about 1/4 block of turquoise clay, make five equal triangles to fit between the star's points, and use an equal amount of turquoise for a flat sheet to wrap around the outside. Then reduce the finished cane to a diameter of about 1/2 inch (1.3 cm).

8. The next cane is a random square assembled from short pieces cut from the canes made so far:

> Two lengths of jellyroll #1, each reduced to 1/4 inch (6 mm) in diameter;
>
> One length of jellyroll #2, 1/2 inch (1.3 cm) in diameter, pressed to flatten;
>
> Two lengths of star cane, 1/2 inch (1.3 cm) in diameter;
>
> Two lengths of flower cane, one 1/2 inch (1.3 cm) and the other reduced to 1/4 inch (6 mm) in diameter;
>
> Two lengthwise slices—one 1/4 inch (6 mm) thick and one 3/8 inch (1 cm) thick—from each striped loaf.

9. Arrange the cane pieces in an overall square shape, alternating them to create an interesting pattern. Once you have an arrangement you like, use both hands to compress all of the canes together. Then cover the complex cane with a light orange sheet made from equal amounts of orange and mother-of-pearl—approximately 1/3 block in total. After wrapping the cane,

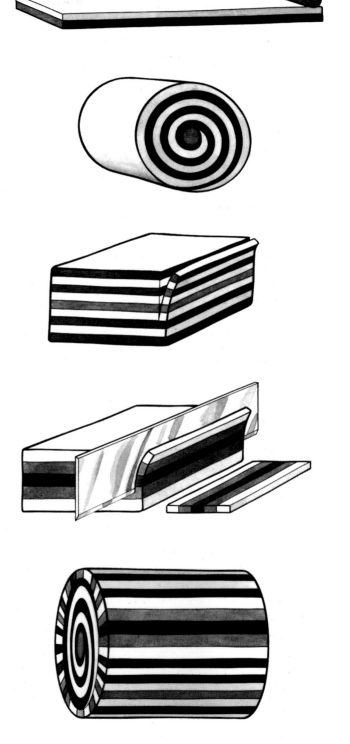

Figure 1

flatten it on all four sides to make a square. Continue to shape with equal pressure on all four sides, reducing the diameter to about 1 inch (2.5 cm) square.

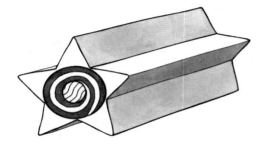

Figure 2

10. The complex circular cane is also assembled from short sections of canes already finished:

   > Two lengths of flower cane, each 3/8 inch (1 cm) in diameter;

   > Two lengths of star cane, each 3/8 inch (1 cm) in diameter;

   > Four lengths of jellyroll #1, each 1/4 inch (6 mm) in diameter.

   Arrange these in an alternating pattern around a mother-of-pearl log. After compressing the components together with your hands, wrap the complex cane with a sheet of yellow clay.

11. Using 1/4 block of yellow and 1/4 block of violet clay, build a six-by-six checkerboard cane. (See page 27 for details.) You'll need 18 individual logs of each color or—if you use the striped loaf method—three sheets of each color. Reduce the finished cane to about 1/2 inch (1.3 cm) in diameter.

12. After finishing all those canes, give yourself a pat on the back! Now you're ready to make some beads. You can use solid colors or scrap clay covered with sheets of the appropriate colors. Make a total of 23 round beads: five white, each 1 inch (2.5 cm); two carmine, each 1-1/8 inch (2.9 cm); four carmine, each 3/4 inch (1.9 cm); four pink, each 3/4 inch (1.9 cm); four violet, each 3/4 inch (1.9 cm); and four violet, each 1 inch (2.5 cm).

13. Cut thin slices from each cane, and apply them randomly to each bead, allowing some of the background of the base beads to show. Roll the beads gently and evenly to blend the slices into the base beads. Then pierce a hole through the center of each bead.

14. Make the spacer beads using a striped loaf consisting of light turquoise, yellow, and carmine. Cut thin slices, and wrap them lengthwise around a log made from scrap clay. Reduce the resulting striped cane to approximately 5/16 inch (8 mm) in diameter, and cut 24 slices, each 1/4 inch (6 mm) thick. Pierce each one so the stripes run lengthwise.

15. With your oven set at 260°F (127°C), bake the spacer beads for about 20 minutes and the larger beads 30 to 35 minutes.

16. When the beads have thoroughly cooled, arrange the round beads in order, placing the largest in the center. String them on nylon thread, alternating round beads with spacer beads. Finish up with a bead tip at each end, add the clasp, and you're ready to hit the town!

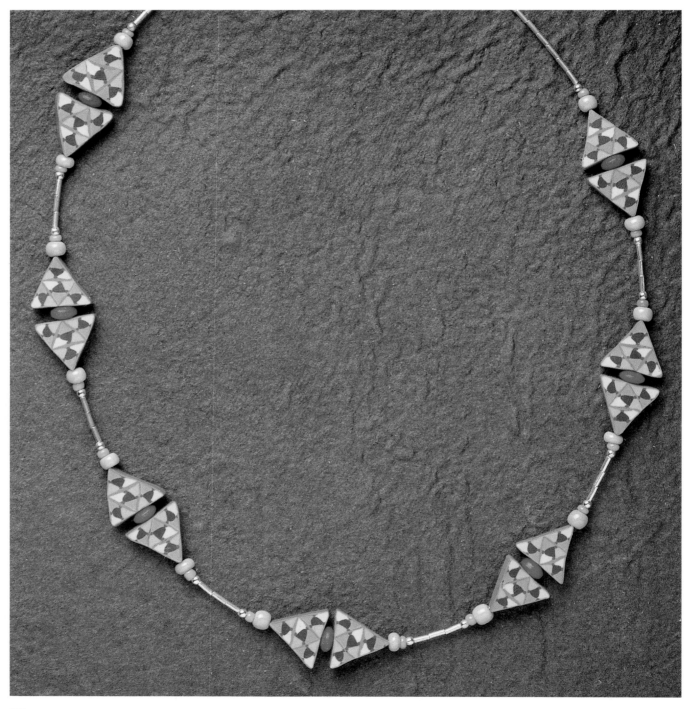

Lively Triangles

Materials

less than 1 block each of yellow,
white, green, blue, red, and purple
Sculpey III
7 - 6 mm red rondelles
14 - 2 mm green glass beads
14 - 5 mm light blue glass beads
14 - 2 mm sterling silver round beads
48 - 1.5 x 4 mm liquid silver beads
tigertail jewelry wire
2 crimps
clasp

Tools

rolling tool
slicing blade
piercing tool
needle-nose pliers or crimping tool

Instructions

1. Begin by mixing the colors you want for the necklace. To make a pale yellow, add a small amount of white to some yellow clay. For a light green, add some green to part of the yellow clay you just mixed. A turquoise shade of blue results from a combination of blue, white, and green. To make the deep, almost black burgundy, add a bit of red to some purple clay. Create a soft lavender by adding some purple to your white clay.

2. From each of the mixed colors—except the lavender—make an individual triangular log about 3 to 3-1/2 inches (7.6 to 8.9 cm) long. Use your fingers or a roller to smooth the sides, and try to make all four logs equal in size.

3. Stack the four logs in a triangular formation, placing the yellow and green on the bottom, burgundy upside-down in the middle, and turquoise at the top. To fill the gaps in the outside edges, make three small logs from red clay. Place one at each corner of the burgundy log.

4. After rolling the lavender clay into a sheet, wrap it around the triangular-shaped cane. Then reduce the cane to about one-quarter its original size. To minimize distortion and help maintain the triangular shape while you're reducing the cane, try to apply even pressure along its length, and turn the triangle frequently as you pinch and pull it.

5. Cut the cane into four equal segments, and restack them into a larger triangle (again place one piece upside-down in the middle). Once you've compressed the segments together with your hands, you can reduce the cane to the size you'd like for your beads.

6. After the cane has rested and cooled, cut a total of 14 slices—each about 1/8 inch (3 mm) thick—for the necklace. Additional slices would make nice earrings. Pierce them through the edges, entering through one point and exiting through the opposite side.

7. Bake all of the beads at 275°F (135°C) for about 15 minutes.

8. When you string the clay beads onto the tigertail, place them in pairs, bottom to bottom, with a red rondelle between them. Between pairs, include the blue, green, and silver round beads and three of the liquid silver beads in the pattern shown in the photograph. When all of the clay beads have been strung, place an equal number of liquid silver beads at each end until the necklace reaches the desired length.

9. Finally, apply the crimps and your clasp.

Alternative Pattern

Using the same basic technique but varying the colors and the pattern of assembly, you can achieve remarkably different effects. The necklace on the following page is a solid strand of "up and down" triangles separated only by small silver beads. The bottom corners of each triangle are gently pulled before baking.

Wish Upon a Star

Materials

1/2 block purple Sculpey III
1 block turquoise brilliant
  Sculpey III
1 block pink brilliant Sculpey
  III
1 block yellow fluorescent
  FIMO
16 - 2.5 mm silver beads
6 - 3 mm silver beads
2 - 5 mm silver beads
144 - 5/32-inch silver tube
  beads
tigertail jewelry wire
2 crimp beads
clasp
2 head pins (optional)
2 French hooks

Tools

rolling tool
slicing blade
toothpicks
piercing tool
needle-nose pliers or
  crimping tool

Instructions

1. Begin by making a bull's-eye cane. For the center, make a log from the purple clay. Then wrap it with a thin sheet of turquoise clay, followed by a sheet of pink clay. As each layer is added, roll the log gently to eliminate any air bubbles.

2. Using your slicing blade, cut a V-shaped wedge along the length of the bull's-eye cane. Then shape a wedge of fluorescent yellow to fit in the gap. (Make sure the FIMO is well conditioned so that its consistency matches that of the Sculpey.) Your fingers work well for general shaping, but to form a distinct wedge, a brayer is the optimal tool. After inserting the yellow wedge, reduce the cane to about 1/2 inch (1.3 cm) in diameter. Then cut the cane into four equal segments.

3. While the canes are resting, roll a log from yellow clay. Arrange the four cane segments around the yellow log, placing them so that their yellow wedges come together in the center to form a four-pointed star (see Figure 1). After compressing the segments together and rolling the cane lightly, cut off a piece about 1 inch (2.5 cm) long, and set it aside for later use.

4. Make a second log of yellow clay. Then reduce the remainder of the star cane to a diameter of about 1/2 inch (1.3 cm), cut it into four pieces, and arrange the segments around the yellow log. Reduce the complex star to a final diameter of about 1/2 inch (1.3 cm).

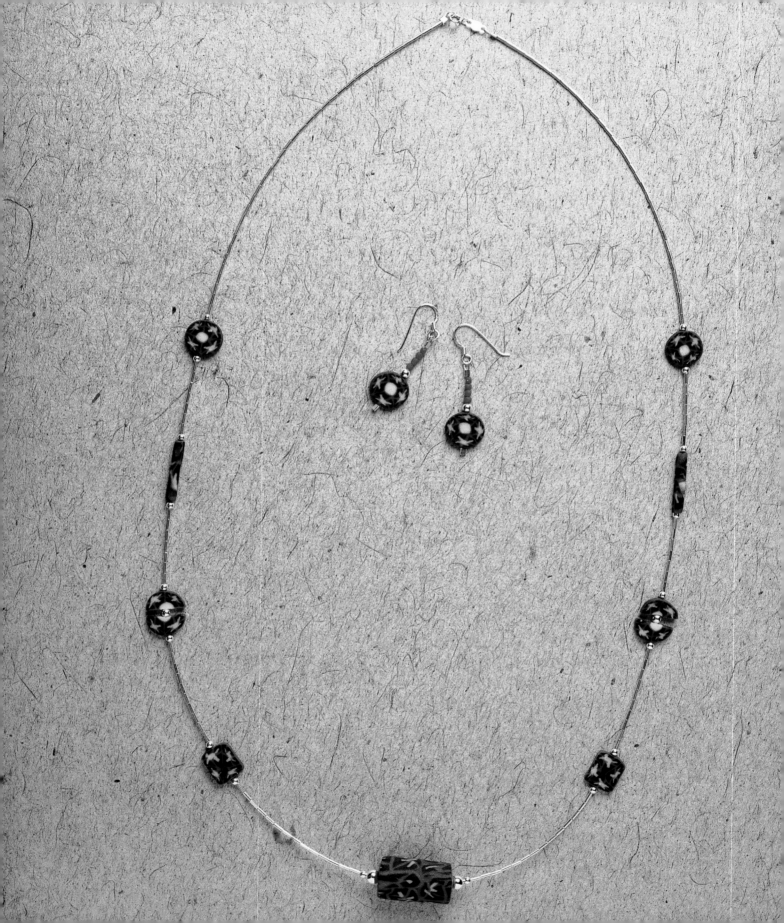

7. To make the tubular beads, use two of the square slices. On each square, trim the edges from two opposite sides, leaving a rectangular-shaped middle section. Place a toothpick on one long edge, and roll the piece lengthwise around the pick, making a tube. To remove the pick, gently twist as you pull it out.

8. For the earrings, you'll also need some bright pink round beads. Roll a log about 1/16 inch (1.6 mm) in diameter, and cut eight or ten small pieces. Using your hands, roll them into round balls about 1/16 inch (1.6 mm) in diameter.

9. Pierce all of the beads, and bake them at 265°F (130°C). The tiny pink beads should bake for about 14 minutes, the star beads for about 16 to 18 minutes, and the largest bead for 20 minutes.
10. To complete the necklace, assemble the beads onto the tigertail as shown in the photo. Crimp the ends, and finish with a clasp.

10. For each earring, thread one circular star bead, a 3 mm silver bead, and four pink clay beads onto a head pin or piece of tigertail finished at the bottom with a crimp. Attach the French hook to a loop in your wire, and your earring is complete.

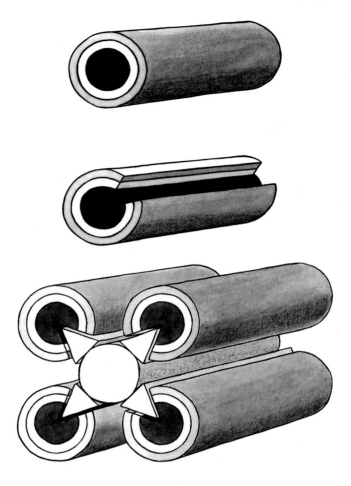

Figure 1

5. Now you're ready to make the beads, starting with the large center bead. Make the base bead using pink clay rolled into a log about 1/2 inch (1.3 cm) in diameter and 1 inch (2.5 cm) long. Using the cane set aside in step 3, cut thin slices and apply them to the pink log. Roll the bead gently to assure good adherence of the slices.

6. Cut the complex star cane (from step 4) into two pieces, and shape one segment into a square cane by rolling or pinching each side. The other segment remains round. Now cut six slices from the round cane (two are for the earrings) and—after it has rested and cooled—four from the square cane. Make each slice about 1/8 inch (3 mm) thick. Cut two of the round slices in half across. Then pierce them through the edges as if the halves were still a complete circle.

BEADS GO BANANAS!

Urban Native

Materials

small amounts of several colors of clay, totaling about 1 block (see below for color formulas)

42 inches (1.1 m) #1 satin cord in coordinating color (add several inches if using #2 cord)

2 - 8 mm jump rings

short length of 20-gauge turquoise niobium wire or purchased clasp

Tools

slicing blade
craft knife
needle-nose pliers
round-nose pliers
wire cutter

Oval   *Spiral*

Large rectangle   *Small rectangle*

Triangle   *End disk*

Connector

Figure 1

Instructions

1. Begin by mixing the colors you'd like to use for your necklace. To replicate those shown here, follow these formulas:

    Light violet - equal parts of neon purple Pro-Mat and Super Sculpey;

    Dark mint green - equal parts of green pearl and white Pro-Mat;

    Medium mint green - equal parts of green pearl Pro-Mat and white Sculpey III;

    Seafoam green - four parts green Pro-Mat, four parts Super Sculpey, and one part white Sculpey III;

    Teal - equal parts blue pearl and green pearl Pro-Mat;

    Salmon - two parts red pearl Pro-Mat, two parts white Sculpey III, and one part yellow Sculpey III;

    Peach - equal amounts of salmon and Super Sculpey;

    Pink - equal parts red pearl Pro-Mat and white Sculpey III;

Dark coral - one part red Pro-Mat, one part yellow Sculpey III, and two parts Super Sculpey;

Sherbet - two parts orange Pro-Mat and one part white Sculpey III;

Sky blue - four parts blue and three parts white Sculpey III.

2. This necklace consists of 13 primary disks of various shapes, and 12 connector disks that are rounded rectangles (see the photo of the reverse side of the necklace). For the connectors, make two each of six different designs. Using sheets of clay about 1/6 inch (1.6 mm) thick, shape the pieces by hand, or cut them with a craft knife to the pattern in Figure 1. The tiny straw from a boxed juice drink is ideal for cutting the stringing holes; just pop each "hole" out of the straw with a toothpick. Make two each of these connector disks:

A: purple Pro-Mat disk with peach "confetti";

B: Light violet with small black triangles;

C: Dark mint green with teal dots;

D: Black Pro-Mat with a slice from a black and white cane; (Use one previously made for another project, or see page 27 for details on making checkerboards.)

E: Peach with medium mint green confetti;

F: Turquoise Pro-Mat with large black triangles.

Apply the designs to one side of the disk between the two stringing holes. "Confetti" is made by rolling a tiny log and cutting short lengths, then pressing the bits randomly onto the disk. To cut triangles, make a thin, flat ribbon of clay. Cut small square pieces, and divide each into two triangles. Dots are made by rolling tiny balls and pressing them onto the disks.

3. The primary disks are slightly thicker—about 1/8 inch (3 mm). Each outer disk also has two stringing holes made with the small straw. See the pattern shapes in Figure 1.

4. The first shape is an end disk made with black Pro-Mat. Decorate this with peach dots scattered randomly.

5. For the second disk, twist two small logs of pink and sherbet together; then repeat with two small logs of seafoam and dark coral. After flattening both twisted logs, form a piece of black Pro-Mat into a log approximately 1-1/2 inches (3.8 cm) long and 3/8 inch (1 cm) wide. Press one flattened cane on top of the black log and the

Figure 2

66

other on the bottom, rolling the assembly lightly between your palms. Now twist the new roll tightly. Flatten this, and shape it into the oval pattern, trimming any excess.

6. Make a small rectangle of black Pro-Mat, and apply a thin slice of a multi-colored star cane on top. (Pages 28–29 have instructions for making star canes.) These stars are made with pink, sky blue, sherbet, and light violet mixed clays, plus yellow and green brilliant Sculpey III.

7. For the fourth disk, make a dark mint triangle. Roll a tiny log of black clay, cut it into short pieces, and apply the dots in a triangular design, pressing them firmly onto the disk.

8. The fifth disk is a spiral pattern made with a thin log about 3-1/4 inch (8.2 cm) long of white Sculpey III placed next to a similar one of black Pro-Mat. Taper the two ends together, and roll them into a spiral, flattening the logs slightly and pressing the edges together as you roll. When the spiral reaches the size of the pattern, cut off the excess.

9. Next combine alternating stripes of teal and peach. Press them together, flatten, and cut the assembly to match the large rectangle pattern.

10. For the middle disk, cut a thick slice from one of your existing canes, and shape it to fit the triangle disk pattern. (This simple stained glass cane consists of squares and rectangles in several colors, each wrapped in a black sheet, stacked together a triangular cane.)

11. Now make a spiral using turquoise Pro-Mat and light violet mixed clay. Turn it upside-down to distinguish it from the other spiral, and add an extra strip of light violet at the bottom for added distinction.

12. The next disk is a slice from a black and white checkerboard cane. If you don't already have one and don't want to make an entire cane, make a checkerboard sheet. To do this, start with one sheet of black and one of white. Cut each lengthwise into strips about 1/8 inch (3 mm) wide. Alternating the colors, reassemble the strips into a single sheet. Then cut the reassembled sheet horizontally into eight strips. Reverse every other row to get the checkerboard, pressing the pieces together with a roller. Then shape the checkerboard to fit the pattern for the large rectangle.

13. For the tenth disk, form a triangle from salmon clay. Top this with black triangles in various sizes, pressing them firmly in place.

14. Now make one medium mint log and one of purple Pro-Mat. Lay the two next to each other, and wind the clay back and forth, giving it a half-twist at each turn. Then flatten it into the oval shape.

15. For the next disk, choose your favorite complex cane. This piece uses international code flags, and each grouping of four spells "love." Cut a slice about 1/8 inch (3 mm) thick, and shape it to fit the small rectangle pattern.

16. For the final disk, shape some light violet clay into the end disk pattern, and decorate it with confetti made from medium mint.

17. Bake all of the disks at 265°F (130°C) for 30 minutes.

18. When all of the pieces have cooled, assemble the primary and connector disks in order for stringing.

19. Prior to stringing, close the jump rings with your needle-nose pliers. Pull one end of the cord through a jump ring until it extends 4-1/2 inches (11.4 cm) on the other side. Holding the two cords together, tie an overhand knot as close to the jump ring as possible. (Note: the remaining three knots use only one cord—the long one. For these, the long cord is tied around the short cord. See Figure 2.) Tie the second knot—a single cord overhand knot—about 1 inch (2.5 cm) from the first. Repeat for the remaining two knots, spacing them as evenly as possible. On the short cord, leave a short "tail" of about 1/4 inch (6 mm), but trim any excess. (Refer to the photos.)

20. To ease threading, place a small dab of white glue at the end of the long cord. (Don't apply glue to the trimmed end, or it will irritate your neck.) Insert the cord from the underside of the first primary disk (an end disk), pulling the cord until the last knot is just touching the corner of the disk. Holding the disk in place with your fingers, thread the cord through the other hole in the disk. Move your hand to hold this section of cord in place while you thread the connector. Continue with the rest of the necklace, placing primary disks on top and connectors on the bottom. Hold each new section in place as you thread to keep the necklace taut but not tight. Once it is completely finished, the necklace will loosen somewhat.

21. When the last end disk has been strung, thread the cord through the remaining jump ring. Measure 6-1/4 inches (15.9 cm) from the tip of

Figure 3

the end disk to the jump ring, and tie an over-hand knot with both cords. Then tie the remaining three knots as previously described, matching the other side of the necklace. Be sure to tie the long cord around the short one, or you will have excess length. Again leave a short tail, and trim any excess.

22. If you are using a purchased clasp, open the jump rings, and attach the two pieces.

23. To make a clasp from niobium wire, cut the wire into one piece about 2 inches (5 cm) long and another about 4 inches (10.2 cm) long. Shape the shorter piece into a loop as shown in Figure 3. Use the tips of your round-nose pliers to make the smaller circle and the wider portions to shape the larger loop, wrapping the end of the wire several times around the middle of the loop. Clip the wire, and file the sharp end.

24. For the hook (see Figure 4), begin with a small loop as before, but extend the wire straight for 1-1/4 inches (3.2 cm). Then bend it sharply back toward the base. Wrap the end several times around the base, clip the excess, and file the end. With the round nose pliers, bend the doubled wire into a hook shape, curving the tip slightly outward.

25. Attach the findings to the jump rings, and your necklace is ready to dazzle your friends.

Figure 4

Served With a Twist

Materials

1-3/4 blocks yellow FIMO
2-1/4 blocks violet FIMO
2-1/2 blocks magenta FIMO
3-1/2 blocks green FIMO
2-3/4 blocks orange FIMO
1/4 block white FIMO
3/4 block dove grey FIMO
1/2 block navy blue FIMO
1/4 block light blue FIMO
1/2 block pink FIMO
2 bead tips
heavy nylon thread
clasp

Tools

rolling tool
slicing blade
piercing tool
beading or darning needle

Instructions

1. Start by making a marbleized log using about 1/8 block each of magenta and green clay. Then flatten 1/4 block of yellow clay into a rectangular sheet as wide as the log is long. Repeat with an equal amount of violet clay. With the yellow sheet on top of the violet and the log placed at one end, roll the clay into a jellyroll with the marbleized log in the center. (See page 55 for an illustration of a similar jellyroll.)

2. Next, using about 1/4 block of each color, make a striped loaf consisting of two layers of magenta alternating with two layers of pink. Then flatten 1/4 block of dove grey into a sheet. After cutting the loaf in half, insert the grey sheet between the two halves so that the magenta layer faces outward on both top and bottom.

3. Make a second striped loaf using 1/4 block each of green and violet. Following the same procedure you used with the first loaf, sandwich a sheet of magenta between two halves of the green and violet cane.

4. Using three or four lengthwise slices from each striped loaf, place the slices so the stripes run lengthwise around the jellyroll. Make sure the slices touch each other all around. Then reduce the cane to a diameter of about 1/2 inch (1.3 cm). This completes jellyroll #1.

5. Following the procedure in step 1, construct jellyroll #2 with a solid green center element wrapped in layers of dove grey and magenta.

6. Again construct two striped loaves as described above. Make the first one with a center of dove grey and alternating layers of violet and yellow. Construct the second with a green center and outer layers of magenta and white.

7. Cover the outside of jellyroll #2 with thin slices of the two striped loaves, and reduce the finished cane to a diameter of about 1/2 inch (1.3 cm).

8. Now cut jellyroll #2 into five equal segments, and place these around a solid green log that is equal in length and of sufficient diameter to allow all five jellyrolls to touch each other. To keep the jellyrolls from shifting, shape a triangular log using green clay, cut it into five segments, and wedge the triangles between the jellyrolls. Then wrap the cane with a sheet of green clay, and reduce the finished cane to about 1/2 inch (1.3 cm) in diameter.

9. For jellyroll #3, use 1/4 block each of orange and magenta, making a simple jellyroll without a center element. After assembly, reduce the cane to about 1/2 inch (1.3 cm) in diameter.

10. Using 1/8 block each of orange and navy blue clay, make a marbleized log. After cutting the log in half, use one segment as the center element for jellyroll #4. Wrap the log in layers of orange and navy, using about 1/8 block of each color.

11. Make another striped loaf as before, this time using pink for the center element and alternating navy and light blue for the outer layers. Cut lengthwise slices from the striped loaf, wrapping them around jellyroll #4 and around the remaining segment of the marbleized log.

12. After compressing and lightly rolling the two canes, cut each one into three equal lengths. Reassemble the segments, grouping the jellyrolls on the inside and placing the marbleized logs in the spaces around the outside. Wrap the assembly in a thick sheet of orange clay. After reducing the cane to about 3/8 inch (1 cm) in diameter, cut six slices about 1/4 inch (6 mm) thick to use for beads. Pierce each one through its edges.

13. Now make a five-pointed star of orange clay, filling in with wedges of yellow, and wrapping the assembly with a sheet of yellow clay. (See pages 28–29 for details on making a star cane.) You'll need about 1/2 block of each color to make a star cane of sufficient size. Then reduce its diameter to about 1/2 inch (1.3 cm).

14. Make a second five-pointed star using yellow for the star and violet for the background and outer sheath. This star has one minor embellishment: wrap a thin sheet of orange around the central yellow log before placing the triangles that form the star. After covering the star with the violet sheath, reduce the cane to a diameter of 1/4 inch (6 mm).

15. For star #3, cut three pieces from star cane #2, each about 2 inches (5 cm) long, stack them together, and wrap the assembly with a sheet of violet clay.

16. Using 1/4 block each of magenta and green clay, make a striped loaf having two layers of each color. Cut the loaf into four segments, and stack them in a parquet pattern (see pages 26–27 for details). Then reduce the cane to approximately 1/2 inch (1.3 cm) in diameter, and cut it in half.

17. Once again build two striped loaves, the first with a center of magenta and outer layers of green and orange. The second should have a green center and outer layers of violet and orange. Each loaf should be a little taller than the parquet cane. Cut four lengthwise slices from the first loaf, and wrap them around one segment of the parquet cane. (See Figure 1.) Similarly, cut four slices from the second loaf, and wrap them around the second piece of parquet cane.

18. Cut each wrapped segment in half again, and stack the four halves so the colors alternate. After compressing the cane together and reducing it to a diameter of about 3/4 inch (1.9 cm), slice two pieces about 1/4 inch (6 mm) thick to use for beads. Pierce them through the edges.

19. To make a flower cane, start with the petals. Using 1/4 block of magenta, roll the clay into a log, and cut it into five equal segments. Using 1/4 block of orange clay, shape five sheets, making each large enough to wrap two-thirds of the way around one of the five petal logs. Then make a center log from 1/8 block of violet clay. Assemble the wrapped petals around the violet center. (See page 28 for an illustration.) Now make five triangular logs using 1/2 block of green clay to wedge between the petals. With 1/4 block of green clay, flatten a sheet to wrap around the entire flower. Then reduce the flower cane to about 1/4 inch (6 mm) in diameter.

20. Using 1/4 block each of magenta and green clay, make a simple four-by-three checkerboard (four squares in each of three rows). The easiest method is to stack four sheets, alternating

Figure 1

colors. Then cut the cane into three segments lengthwise, and flip the middle segment to make a checkerboard. (See page 27 for more details.) Reduce the finished cane until it is about 1/2 inch (1.3 cm) high.

21. To make the random square cane used in this necklace, begin by making one final striped loaf. Following the same procedures described previously, make the loaf with an orange center and alternating layers of yellow and violet. Then cut two lengthwise slices about 1/4 inch (6 mm) thick.

22. Assemble the random cane using segments from several of the canes already made. Place jellyroll #3 roughly in the center, and surround it with two segments of jellyroll #2, two of star cane #2, the two lengthwise slices from the layered bar completed in the previous step, one segment of star cane #3, and one of the flower cane. When the canes are arranged to your liking, compress them together into a square loaf. Then, using a roller or your hands, reduce the complex loaf to a diameter of about 1 inch (2.5 cm). Cut two slices 1/4 inch (6 mm) thick to use for beads, and pierce them diagonally through their edges.

23. Now assemble a round complex cane. Take about half of jellyroll #1 and reduce it to 1/4 inch (6 mm) in diameter. Then cut the reduced cane into three equal segments. Cut three segments from the flower cane, and arrange these in an alternating pattern with the jellyroll segments around an orange log in the center.

Using 1/4 block of magenta, flatten a sheet large enough to wrap around the complex cane. Then compress all of the elements together with your hands. After reducing the cane to 1/2 inch (1.3 cm) in diameter, cut eight slices about 1/4 inch (6 mm) thick to use as beads. To give them a more abstract appearance, pinch or squeeze the wafer-shaped beads until they are no longer perfectly circular.

24. With all of the canework behind you, now you're ready for the easy part. Using either solid green or scrap clay covered with a layer of green, form a total of eight round balls. Make two balls 1-1/8 inch (about 3 cm) in diameter, two 1 inch (2.5 cm), two 3/4 inch (about 2 cm), and two 5/8 inch (about 1.5 cm). Form a ninth ball from magenta clay, making it 1-3/8 inch (3.5 cm) in diameter. Using thin slices cut from each cane, apply the designs randomly to each bead, allowing some of the background to show. Then pierce each bead through the center.

25. Take one of the 1-1/8-inch (3 cm) beads in both hands, and press it slightly to flatten it somewhat. Then twist the bead in opposite directions (i.e., the right hand pushes forward and the left pushes back). Use gentle but steady pressure to avoid tearing the clay. Repeat with the other matching bead. (Note: In order to keep the hole centered, it's easier to pierce the bead first, before shaping it.)

26. Form the two 3/4-inch (2 cm) beads into elongated ovals and the largest (center) bead into a rounded rectangular shape.

27. Make two small spacer beads by forming scrap bits of magenta, orange, and violet clay into round balls 1/8 inch (3 mm) in diameter. When the colors have swirled into a pattern you like, pierce the beads through the center.

28. Bake all of the beads at 260°F (127°C). The smaller beads should remain in the oven about 20 minutes, the medium-sized beads for 30 minutes, and the largest beads for 40 minutes.

29. Thread the beads onto the heavy nylon, placing the large rectangular bead in the center, and alternating small beads and other large ones on each side. Finish the ends with fold-over bead tips, and attach your clasp. Congratulations! It was a lengthy process, but you now have a stylish piece of jewelry that will draw admiring glances whenever you wear it.

Watch Faces

Materials

2 blocks black Pro-Mat (recommended for its added strength)
previously constructed face cane (see pages 29–30)
remnants of various simple canes
black round elastic
white glue
watch face (with pins to attach band)

Tools

2 darning needles and some scrap clay made into a double piercing tool (see below)
slicing blade
rolling tool (optional)
toothpick

Instructions

1. Before starting your watch band, make a simple tool for piercing two holes simultaneously into each bead. Place two darning needles side by side, about 1/4 inch (6 mm) apart, and encase the ends in some scrap clay formed into a handle. Bake your double piercing tool at 275°F (135°C) for about 20 minutes.

2. For the band itself, first measure the circumference of your wrist. Then subtract the length of your watch face (the distance from one pin to the other), and divide the remainder by the diameter you plan to make each bead. (This band uses beads that are about 3/8 inch or 1 cm in diameter.) Now you know how many beads you'll need for your band. If you end up with a fraction, adjust the diameter of each bead accordingly.

3. Roll the black Pro-Mat into a log the diameter you want for each bead, and cut it into as many segments as you calculated above. Be sure to cut the segments equal in length to make your beads uniform. When sizing the beads, take into account the dimensions of your watch face. To make the beads, you can either round the ends of your cut segments, or you can roll each into a ball and form the ball into a short log with rounded ends.

4. Reduce part of your face cane to a diameter of about 1/2 inch (1.3 cm), and further reduce some to about 3/8 inch (1 cm) in diameter. The difference in size will give variety to your beads. To decorate the beads, cut thin slices of the face cane and apply them to the top sides of about one-third of your beads. Add "hair"—actually slices of jellyrolls, stripes, or triangular bull's eyes.

5. For the other beads, use various stripes, jelly-rolls, checkerboards, and other simple canes to make pleasing designs. This band uses mainly black and white patterns, plus a smattering of blue designs for extra punch. Slices of canes can be used as is or cut into smaller sections to collage together into decorative elements. Gently press the cane slices onto the beads, or use a roller to smooth the designs onto the bead surfaces. Don't be dismayed if your beads are no longer exactly the same size and shape once you've applied your decorative canes. Minor variations are not only artful, they may be helpful for getting a good fit around your wrist.

6. After the beads have rested and cooled, pierce two holes into each one using the double piercing tool. Be careful to line up the holes so that the beads will be in line when strung. Then, using a toothpick, enlarge all the holes to accommodate the thickness of the elastic. On the two beads that will adjoin the watch face, make the holes large enough to allow the elastic to be doubled back through each hole to form a loop.

7. To bake the beads, first preheat your oven to 300°F (149°C). When you place the beads into the oven, turn off the heat. Leave the beads in for about 30 minutes to bake in the gradually decreasing temperature.

8. String the beads onto two pieces of elastic, placing the beads with the larger holes at either end. Detach the pins from the watch face, and loop the elastic over the pins and back through the end beads. Before gluing, replace the pins onto the watch face, and test the watch and band together for fit. Add, subtract, or substitute beads as necessary. Once the band is comfortable, detach the pins again, and glue the elastic into each end bead. When the glue is dry, trim off any excess elastic, and reattach the watch face. Then beware of watch thieves!

Heart's Desire

Materials

1 block black Sculpey III
1 block white Sculpey III
1/2 block red Sculpey III
1/2 block green Sculpey III
1/2 block purple Sculpey III
1/2 block yellow Sculpey III
1 block blue Sculpey III
tigertail jewelry wire
*32 - 4 mm round sterling
   silver beads*
*32 - 3 mm round sterling
   silver beads*
*26 - 2 x 4 mm silver tube
   beads*
30 - 6 mm Czech glass beads
2 crimp beads
clasp
2 head pins
2 ear wires

Tools

rolling tool
slicing blade
piercing tool
*needle-nose pliers or
   crimping tool*

Instructions

1. Begin with the center pattern of the cane beads, and make a simple black and white striped loaf using four layers of each color. Maintaining the square form, reduce the cane until you can easily cut it into four equal segments. Use your roller or fingers to keep the edges flat and corners sharp as the cane elongates. After cutting, stack the parts in a parquet pattern (see pages 26–27 for details), and add a tiny red log at the center of each side of the parquet where the cane segments come together.

2. After mixing your colors, if desired, flatten a total of eight sheets of clay: two each of green, purple, yellow, and red. Make each sheet as long as the cane and wide enough to wrap all the way around it. Alternating the colors, wrap each sheet around the cane, butting the edges and trimming any excess. Gently roll the cane with the addition of each sheet to compress the elements together. Finally, cut the cane into three segments, stack them, and reduce the assembly to a finished diameter of about 3/4 inch (1.9 cm).

3. After allowing the cane to rest and cool, cut 15 slices, each about 1/4 inch (6 mm thick). Then coax each one into a heart shape using your fingers. Work slowly, and use gentle pressure to form the clay into the desired shapes.

4. Choosing different locations on some of the hearts, pierce all of the slices through the edges.

5. To make each snail bead, roll a log of blue clay that is about 2 inches (5.1 cm) long. The log should be thick in the center and taper gently to the ends, where it is about one-eighth the diameter. Coil up both ends until they meet in the middle. Bending them slightly apart, place the two coils next to one another, and press them gently together to adhere. This completes your snail bead. Once you've mastered the technique, make 15 additional snails the same size. Then pierce each one through the crease between the coils.

6. Bake all of the beads at 275°F (135°C) for about 15 minutes.

7. When cool, assemble the beads onto the tigertail. Begin the necklace with a small silver bead, and follow with several silver tube beads. In the repeat pattern, each heart and snail bead is surrounded by a three-bead sequence: a large silver bead, a Czech bead, and another large silver bead. Reverse the initial sequence at the end so that the small silver bead is the final one.

8. Make the earrings next. On each head pin, mount a heart bead, a large silver bead, a snail bead, another large silver bead, a Czech bead, and one small silver bead. Form the top of the head pin into a loop, and attach it to the ear wires.

Stained Glass Effects

Materials

4 blocks black Sculpey III
4 blocks translucent Sculpey III
1/4 block red Sculpey III
1/2 block orange Sculpey III
3/4 block pink brilliant Sculpey III
1/2 block yellow Sculpey III
1 block blue Sculpey III
1-1/4 blocks white Sculpey III
tigertail jewelry wire
2 crimp beads
black or white round elastic cord
4 head pins
2 earring backs
glue

Tools

rolling tool
clay extruder (recommended)
slicing blade
wooden skewer
piercing tool

Instructions

Here translucent clay is used to create the effect of stained glass. The bright colors of the base beads show through the "leaded glass patterns" that are created by slices of a cane made from translucent and black clay. This project is ideal for those who like to experiment and enjoy making abstract patterns.

1. Begin making a rectangular loaf from the bottom up. Start with a layer of black shapes, then a layer of translucent shapes, utilizing positive and negative space to form a pattern. Use round, triangular, and square logs, jellyrolls, wavy sheets, and other shapes to build up your cane, alternating layers of black and translucent clay. Using a clay extruder makes this process easier. To get plenty of variety without using vast amounts of clay, make your loaf large in cross section (tall and wide) but short in length. While you're building the loaf, try to maintain an overall rectangular shape. See Figure 1.

2. When you're satisfied with your cane, divide it in half. Using a roller, reduce one segment until it is about half the diameter of the original cane. This is to give more variety to your beads.

3. While the canes are resting, mix the colors for the base beads. Red clay is made from 1/4 block of red mixed with 1/2 block of orange and 1/4 block of pink brilliant. To get orange, mix equal amounts of yellow and pink brilliant. Lighten the blue slightly by adding a small amount of white (about five parts blue to one part white).

4. Make logs from each color for the base beads. These can be cut into short, medium, and longer lengths for beads of varying shapes and dimensions. (Some will be curved into arcs and others into rings after the cane slices have been applied.) Form a few round beads, and cut some thick square slices. At the same time, make several disks, barrels, and small round beads of various solid colors to use as spacers between the decorated beads.

5. Once you have a selection of bead shapes you like, cut very thin slices from each cane, and wrap them around the brightly colored base beads. For added interest, wrap the cane slices at varying angles and directions. Don't worry if the bright colors of the base beads don't show through; the translucency of the clay doesn't become obvious until it has been baked.

6. Now curve some of the longer log-shaped beads into arcs and circles. If you like, cut one or two of the round beads in half. Let your imagination be your guide.

7. Pierce all of the beads except those for the earrings with the wooden skewer. Pierce those with a smaller tool. The rings obviously don't need holes; they will float freely on the necklace.

Figure 1

8. Bake the beads at 250°F (120°C) for about 45 minutes.

9. String the beads for the necklace onto the tigertail, alternating shapes and base colors. Periodically, slip a ring onto the necklace. To make this a continuous necklace (without a clasp), insert one end of the tigertail through both crimp beads and into one or two beads beyond the crimps. Then insert the other end of the tigertail through the crimps from the opposite direction, extending it through one or two beads as well. Pull the necklace snug, and squash the crimps with your pliers. The crimps are small enough to slide into the holes in the beads and disappear. Trim the excess tigertail.

10. For the bracelet, cut your elastic long enough to provide several inches extra at each end. Thread the beads onto the cord, reserving those with the largest holes for the ends. After stringing enough beads to fit completely around your wrist, tie a double knot with the elastic.

11. The earrings consist of two parts: the post and the dangle. The post is simply a flat, square bead threaded onto a head pin. The head pin is finished with a loop to interlock with the one on the dangle. The dangle is formed by threading a selection of beads onto a head pin and securing them with a loop at the top. Connect the dangles with the posts, glue on the findings, and your earrings are complete.

Trip Around the World

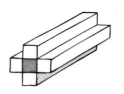
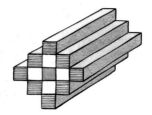

Materials

graph paper
1 block orange FIMO
1 block yellow FIMO
1 block green FIMO
2 blocks purple FIMO
2 blocks light turquoise
  FIMO
1 block pink FIMO
2 blocks white FIMO
3 blocks black FIMO
heavy nylon thread
28 - 3 mm black beads

Tools

rolling tool
clay extruder (optional)
slicing blade
toothpicks
piercing tool
beading or darning needle

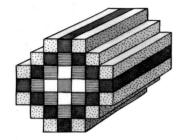

Instructions

1. Begin your necklace by deciding upon the colors for your quilt pattern. Using graph paper and colored pencils, experiment with different combinations until you have one that you especially like.

2. To build the quilt pattern shown here ("trip around the world"), you'll need to construct a total of 49 square logs. To do this more easily, you can flatten the clay into thick sheets. Then cut each strip as wide as it is thick. Alternatively, you can form the logs with a clay extruder. To complete the pattern as shown in the photo, make the following logs: one orange, eight yellow, eight green, 12 purple, 12 light turquoise, and eight pink. (Save some of your clay for the matching bull's-eye pattern.)

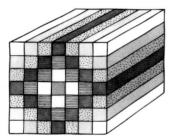

3. An optional step is to wrap each log with a very thin layer of black clay, as shown in this piece. This gives the pattern more contrast and makes the colors more dramatic, but the design looks fine without it.

4. When you have all of the logs complete, build the overall square loaf from the bottom up according to your grid, or from the center outward as shown in Figure 1.

5. Now make an additional 50 bars for the border pattern: 25 white and 25 black. Alternating the two colors, use these to cover the quilt-patterned cane. Then wrap the entire cane with a very thin sheet of black clay.

6. Following the same color sequence you chose for your quilt pattern, create a bull's-eye cane (see page 24 for details). Again, wrap the completed cane in a thin sheet of black clay.

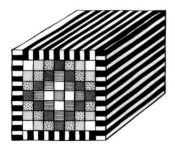

Figure 1

80

7. After reducing the square loaf to about 1-1/2 inches (3.8 cm) in diameter, cut three slices—each about 1/8 inch (3 mm) thick—for the base of the pectoral piece. Arrange the slices in a gentle curve as shown in the photo, overlapping the corners. When you have the slices attractively placed, press the corners together gently with your fingers. To make the loops that will be used to attach the pectoral to the rest of the necklace, turn over the farthest corner at each end, folding it back to make a loop. Place a toothpick into each opening to keep the overlap from being pressed together.

8. Now gradually reduce both canes, cutting slices at several sizes to use to embellish the pectoral. Cut slices about 1/16 inch (1.6 mm) thick, and press them into various locations on the three larger squares, creating a collage of patterns. For bits of bright color, make a few small balls of each color, and press them onto the slices. Indent the centers using a rounded pencil eraser or other small object.

9. When both canes have been reduced to about 5/8 inch (1.6 cm) in diameter, cut 12 square slices and 13 bull's eyes for beads, making each slice about 1/4 inch (6 mm) thick. Using an instrument large enough to make a hole that will accommodate two thicknesses of your nylon thread, pierce all of the beads through their edges.

10. Setting your oven at 250°F (120°C), bake all of the beads and the pectoral piece for about one hour.

11. Begin stringing your necklace at the pectoral. For each half of the necklace, thread the nylon cord through one flap, and bring both ends of the nylon through each bead. Alternate round black beads with the squares and bull's eyes. At one end, make a fastener by tying a sequence of knots in your thread and looping the knots around into a circle. At the other end, use three black beads to separate one bull's eye for your button, and tie off your string before and after the polymer bead.

Fresh Fruits

Materials

(For each fruit, less than 1/2 block of each color is needed.)

lime: green, leaf green, yellow, and white FIMO

lemon: yellow, golden yellow, and white FIMO

orange: orange, golden yellow, yellow, and white FIMO

grapes: magenta, violet, white, leaf green, and terra cotta FIMO

pineapple: golden yellow, terra cotta, caramel, yellow, green, leaf green, and white FIMO

head pins

ear wires or French hooks

pin backs

Tools

rolling tool
slicing blade
piercing tool

Instructions

1. Each citrus fruit is made from one jellyroll (see pages 24–25 for more details). Depending on which fruit you plan to make, stack the layers accordingly:

   Orange: orange, golden yellow, orange, yellow;

   Lemon: yellow, golden yellow, yellow;

   Lime: green, leaf green, green, yellow.

   With your fingers or a roller, flatten one end of the stack into a wedge, and cut the other end on an angle so that the bottom sheets slightly overextend the top ones. Roll from the wedge end to form the jellyroll.

2. Flatten a piece of white clay into a thin sheet large enough to fit exactly around the jellyroll. After wrapping the sheet around the jellyroll, reduce the cane until you can easily cut it into eight equal sections.

3. Arrange the eight sections in a ring. Then, holding the assembly in both hands, gently compress the ring from all sides until there is no longer a

space in the center. Although some unevenness looks realistic, your goal is to compress the sections equally.

4. For the skin of your fruit, choose the appropriate color—orange, golden yellow, or green—and make a sheet large enough to cover the cane. Gauge the thickness of the skin based on the size of your cane, and wrap it around the cane. For a more finished look, apply a thick sheet of white clay over the cane to "frame" the fruit.

5. If you've made a few different citrus fruits, stack them together before slicing. To make the fruit charms, cut slices about 1/8 inch (3 mm) thick and pierce them through the edges.

6. Bake the slices at 225˚F (107˚C) for about 12 to 20 minutes, depending on the size of your pieces.

7. For the grapes, make a jellyroll following the same procedure described above, stacking a layer of violet, one of magenta, and another of violet to make the jellyroll. Then reduce the jellyroll until it can be cut into 14 equal sections.

8. Using a small amount of white clay, roll a long, thin log about half the diameter of the purple jellyroll. With your fingers or a roller, form the log into a triangular shape. Then cut it into ten sections about the same length as those cut from the jellyroll.

9. Arrange the jellyroll pieces into two rows of four, one row of three, one row of two, and one jellyroll at the bottom. Fill in the negative space around the grapes by placing a white triangular section in each space between jellyrolls except at the top center where the stem will be. (See Figure 1.)

10. For the leaves, make a simple jellyroll using leaf green for the bottom layer and a smaller amount of terra cotta clay for the top layer. Form the two layers into a jellyroll, and cut it into two equal sections. Place the sections side by side, and pinch along the top, joining the two rolls into one triangular-shaped roll. Then cut this cane into three sections.

11. Roll a second log of white clay, and form it into a tall, thin triangle, about the same height as the green and brown cane. Make the log long enough to cut it into two sections equal in length to the cane sections.

12. Arrange the three sections of green and brown cane into a clover shape, and fill the negative space with the white triangles. You now have

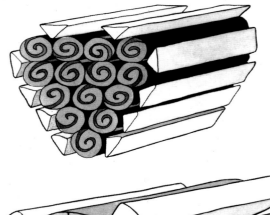

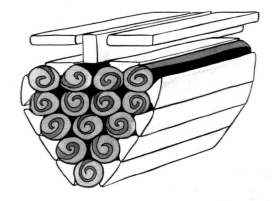

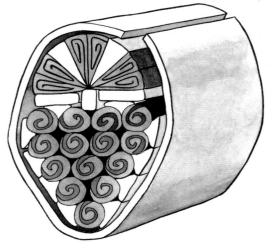

Figure 1

83

grape leaves. At this point, compare the size of these leaves with your grape cluster. If the cane is too large, reduce it by gently squeezing and manipulating it with your hands.

13. Make a stem using scraps of green and terra cotta clay, kneading the two colors together to make a rectangular log. Place it on top of the grape cluster as shown in Figure 1.

14. Flatten a piece of white clay into a sheet about 1/8 inch (3 mm) thick. With your blade, cut it into two pieces as long as the canes and about as wide as half the grape cluster. Place these on either side of the stem, and position the leaf assembly on top.

15. To finish, flatten a sheet of white clay. This will form a border around the fruit cluster, so make it as thick or as thin as you want. Compress the assembly together with both hands, and work it gently until it is the size you like.

16. Cut slices for charms, or make pins by cutting thinner slices and applying them to slabs of colorful clay. Pierce and bake as described above.

17. To make a pineapple, construct a jellyroll cane as previously described. Use golden yellow on the bottom, followed by terra cotta, caramel, and yellow. After forming the jellyroll, reduce the cane to a length sufficient to make ten equal sections. Assemble the pineapple by placing two sections in the top row, three in the middle two rows, and two in the bottom row. Then compress the components together lightly.

18. For the leaves, form two long, narrow, wedge-shaped logs, one green and one leaf green. Then make an identical pair of long, narrow wedges using white clay. Placing thick edges on top of thin ones, interleave the wedges: first white, then green, then white, and finally leaf green. The thick ends of the green and leaf green wedges should touch. See Figure 2. Using your hands to work the material, reduce the cane until it is four times as long as the pineapple body. Then cut it into four sections, putting two sections together back-to-back so that the green sides touch. Put the other two sections together the same way, and stack one set on top of the other. Press the entire construction onto the pineapple body, bending the sections slightly to form pleasing leaf shapes. Use extra pieces of white clay as needed to make the leaves take the shape you want.

19. Finally, flatten a sheet of white clay—as thin or as thick as you like—to wrap around the pineapple for a border.

20. After cutting slices, pierce and bake them as described above.

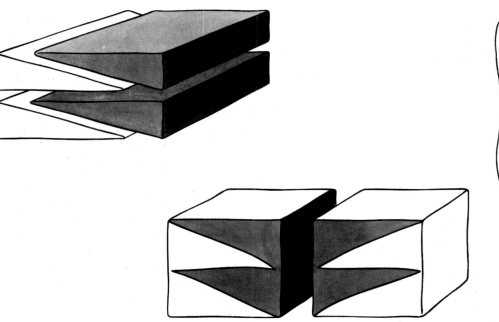

Figure 2

Button Covers to Match

Materials

1 block yellow Sculpey III
1 block white Sculpey III
1 block pink brilliant Sculpey
   III
1 block purple Sculpey III
small amount of red Sculpey
   III
button cover backs
glue

Tools

rolling tool
slicing blade
parchment paper

Instructions

1. Using a round cane in any pattern you like, you can make button covers to match your favorite outfit. This simple flower has a yellow center with fuchsia petals. To make one that is similar, start by mixing some magenta and fuchsia clay. Add a small amount of red to some pink brilliant clay for the magenta. For fuchsia, use part of your magenta clay, and add some white.

2. Start your flower with the center. Roll the yellow clay into a log, and flatten the magenta clay into a sheet large enough to wrap once around the log. Butt the edges at the joint, trimming off any excess. Then reduce the resulting bull's eye to about one-fifth its original diameter. After cutting the cane into five equal segments, stack the pieces together into a single cane.

3. Now roll the fuchsia clay into one or more logs (all the same diameter) to make six petals. Place these evenly around the flower center. Using the purple clay, make triangle-shaped logs that can be cut into segments and fitted between the fuchsia petals. Then wrap the flower assembly in a sheet of purple. Reduce the flower until you can easily cut it into seven segments. After reassembling the pieces into a complex cane, reduce the finished pattern to the diameter of your button covers.

4. Cut very thin slices, and place them on a sheet of oven parchment. Bake the slices with your oven set at 275°F (135°C), checking for doneness every five minutes.

5. When the slices have cooled, glue them onto the button covers.

Oriental Overture

Materials

1-1/4 blocks mother-of-pearl
 FIMO
1-1/4 blocks bronze FIMO
1-1/4 blocks anthracite
 FIMO
pin back
glue
8 - 3 mm brown glass beads
2 head pins
2 earring post backs

Tools

rolling tool
slicing blade
craft knife

Instructions

1. To begin the kimono pin, flatten 1/4 block of each color of clay into a square sheet. Then stack the sheets, placing the mother-of-pearl between the anthracite and bronze, and trim the edges to make a square loaf.

2. Cut the stack lengthwise into four sections, and layer the segments so that the order—anthracite, pearl, bronze—is maintained.

3. Now divide the cane into four equal pieces, stacking these in a parquet pattern (see pages 26–27 for more details). Then reduce the cane to a diameter of about 1/2 inch (1.3 cm).

4. Using 1/8 block of each color, make another three-layered stack of anthracite, pearl, and bronze. Form this into a jellyroll, and reduce its diameter to about 1/4 inch (6 mm).

5. With equal amounts of bronze and mother-of-pearl (about 1/8 block of each), combine the clays to make a tan color. Flatten the tan clay into a rectangular sheet. Using 1/4 block each of anthracite and bronze, flatten these two colors into sheets close in size to the tan layer. Then stack the three, and trim the edges to make a rectangular, striped loaf.

6. Combine all of your scrap pieces, and flatten this material into a sheet about 1/8 inch (3 mm) thick to use as a backing for the kimono pin.

7. To assemble your kimono, place your slices first; then cut the final T-shape according to the pattern in Figure 1. Begin with the sleeves. Each is two slices from the parquet-patterned cane. These are separated by a lengthwise slice from the striped cane, which forms the front opening of the kimono. On each side below each sleeve,

three more slices from the parquet pattern are placed. Smooth the slices together and blend the seams with your roller. Using your craft knife, cut the outline of the kimono.

8. For the obi, lay a second slice from the striped cane across the kimono just below the sleeves. Finish this with four slices from the jellyroll cane. Smooth the obi with your roller.

9. When you're satisfied with its appearance, bake the pin at 200°F (93°C) for 30 to 40 minutes.

10. After it has cooled, glue the pin back in position.

11. For the earrings, cut the remainder of your jelly-roll into three segments. Wrap one portion (jellyroll #1) in a thin sheet of anthracite clay. With a much thicker sheet of anthracite clay, wrap the second segment (jellyroll #2). Reduce the third portion (jellyroll #3) to a diameter of about 1/8 inch (3 mm).

12. To make the square bead at the top of each earring, assemble a striped cane and a solid log to combine with jellyroll #1. Using about 1/8 block of material for each sheet, flatten two sheets of mother-of-pearl and one each of bronze and anthracite, trimming each into a square. Stack the sheets in this order: pearl, bronze, pearl, anthracite. Then slice the resulting cane into two segments, placing one on top of another to double the pattern. After compressing the striped cane into a rectangle about 1/4 inch (6 mm) high, slice it into four sections, and arrange them around jellyroll #1. (Refer to the photo for placement.) Then combine two parts mother-of-pearl with one part bronze clay to make light tan. Using the light tan clay, roll four square logs to fit into the corners of the cane. After compressing the cane together and reducing it to the size desired, cut two slices, about 1/4 inch (6 mm) thick, for the earring tops. Do not pierce these.

Figure 1

13. Slice two pieces of jellyroll #2 for the first dangles, piercing each through its edges.

14. For the second dangle, build a square, striped loaf consisting of two sheets each of mother-of-pearl and bronze, alternating the colors. Make the cane approximately equal in length to jellyroll #3. Then cut several thin, lengthwise slices from the striped loaf, and wrap these around jellyroll #3. After reducing the resulting cane to a diameter of about 1/4 inch (6 mm), cut two slices for the dangles. Pierce these through their edges.

15. The last dangles are simply square logs of anthracite clay, about 3/4 inch (1.9 cm) long and 1/4 inch (6 mm) square. Pierce these lengthwise.

16. Bake all of the earring beads at 200°F (93°C) for about 30 minutes.

17. Glue the earring posts to the square beads, and assemble the dangles onto the head pins, alternating the polymer beads with the glass beads as shown in the photo. Using pliers, bend the tops of the head pins into loops, and slip the loops over the posts of the earring backs. This arrangement allows you to wear the posts with or without dangles, depending on your mood.

Starburst

Materials

1-1/2 blocks white FIMO
1 block black FIMO
1-1/2 blocks light blue FIMO
1-1/2 blocks violet FIMO
1/2 block yellow FIMO
1/2 block red FIMO
1/2 block turquoise FIMO
1/2 block mint FIMO
1/8-inch (3 mm) diameter
    aluminum tubing, about
    15 inches (38.1 cm) long
34 small eye hooks
56 - 6 mm black glass beads
tigertail jewelry wire
2 crimp beads
clasp

Tools

rolling tool
slicing blade
ruler or straightedge
craft knife

Instructions

1. Build the first of two triangular striped canes by assembling the layers you'll need: eight of white and eight of light blue sheathed on both sides with violet. Make the light blue and white layers about twice as thick as the violet ones. It is easier to work with the stripes if you preassemble the blue and violet sheets into "sandwiches" and treat them as single units.

2. Starting with a violet-jacketed blue stripe, build your triangle from the bottom up, alternating the layers. By diminishing the width of each stripe, you can create the basic shape of the triangle as you assemble it. Compress the layers together with your roller as you stack them. To make your cane a perfect triangle, trim the sides with your blade.

3. When the triangular cane is fully assembled, wrap it first in a sheet of violet clay, then in a sheet of black. Then, with a roller or your fingers, reduce the cane until the bottom side is about 1 inch (2.5 cm) wide, turning it frequently as you reduce it to keep the pattern from distorting.

4. Make the second triangular cane a little more complicated than the first. Moving from the bottom up, start with a sheet of black clay. Follow this with a sheet of violet and another of black, making all three layers equal in thickness. This makes the bottom component of the first layer of the cane.

5. For the next section, the easiest way to make all of the vertical elements consistent is to build a striped loaf as tall as your triangular cane is wide. Then trim it to the dimensions you want. Alternate layers of light blue with layers of yellow, separating each with a sheet of black. After trimming the edges of the loaf, cut a lengthwise slice the appropriate thickness for your cane. Place this so the stripes run vertically across your triangle.

6. Now add three flat sheets: black, violet, and black.

7. Form a second striped loaf using about 13 layers each of red and white clay, separating each with a thin sheet of black. After compressing the layers together and trimming the edges, cut a lengthwise slice, and stack it on your triangular cane.

8. Follow this with a layer of mint and one of turquoise clay.

9. For the third striped loaf, use yellow and violet. Alternate the colors, and separate each as before with a sheet of black clay. Cut a lengthwise slice of this bar, and stack it on your triangular cane.

10. Add another sheet of turquoise and one of mint clay.

11. Finish the top of the triangle with layers of white and light blue as you did for the first cane. Then wrap the cane in a sheet of violet followed by one of black, as you did the first cane. Trim and reduce the cane until it closely matches the first one in size.

12. After both canes have rested and cooled, cut eight slices from the first (simpler) cane and nine slices from the second one. Each slice should be about 1/8 inch (3 mm) thick.

13. Screw two eye hooks into the bottom edge of each slice, placing them a uniform distance apart on each triangle. Inset the eye hooks a short distance from the outer corners as shown in photograph.

14. Bake all of the slices—with hooks installed—at 250°F (120°C) for about 30 minutes.

15. String the necklace as shown in the photo, threading the tigertail through the eye hooks, and cutting the aluminum tubing to fit each slice. Use three black glass beads as spacers between each polymer triangle.

16. Finish by crimping the tigertail and attaching a clasp.

Abstract Expression

Materials

1 block fluorescent yellow
   FIMO
1 block metallic blue Sculpey
   III
1/2 block black Sculpey III
1/4 block nightglow FIMO
1/8 block red brilliant
   Sculpey III
sheet of vellum or wax paper
pin back
12 - 3 mm sterling silver
   beads
tigertail jewelry wire
2 crimp beads
clasp

Tools

rolling tool
slicing blade
piercing tool
needle-nose pliers or
   crimping tool

Instructions

1. To obtain the colors used for the abstract cane, mix the two main colors, making sure the FIMO has been conditioned to the same consistency as the Sculpey III:

    Blue: 3/4 block metallic blue and 1/4 block fluorescent yellow;

    Yellow: 1/2 block fluorescent yellow and one marble-sized ball of metallic blue.

2. Abstract patterns are just that—abstract. To create your own unique design, simply combine several small logs and other shapes until you have a pleasing arrangement. This one is made from a total of ten blue logs, seven yellow logs, three sheets of blue clay and two of yellow. As shown in Figure 1, the individual components vary in size and configuration.

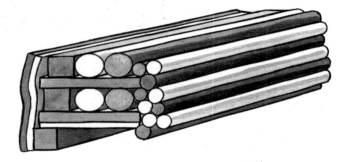

Figure 1

3. Wrap your abstract blue and yellow cane with a sheet of black clay, and roll it gently to compress everything together. Cut the cane in half, setting one piece aside. Reduce the other to a diameter about half the size of the reserved cane. Then squeeze the reduced cane on two sides, transforming it into a football shape. After cutting the football-shaped cane into three segments that are equal in length, flatten one piece completely until it is about 1/8 inch (3 mm) thick.

4. Using the larger cane set aside in the previous step, press this cane into a football shape, and cut it into two pieces. Then combine all four football-shaped segments and the flattened one into a single cane. Use your roller to flatten each side of the cane into a square loaf about 1/2 inch (1.3) cm on each side.

5. To make the "sprocket holes" (reminiscent of a piece of photographic film) on each end of the pin, begin with a log of nightglow clay. Using a roller, square the log. Then wrap the log in a sheet of black clay, again using the roller to retain the square shape. Cut the wrapped cane into four equal segments, and stack them vertically. Reduce the completed cane, if necessary, until it is about 1-1/4 inch (3.2 cm) high.

6. To make the rich purple clay for the backing of the pin and the edges of the sprocket holes, mix equal parts of red brilliant and metallic blue. You'll need only about 1/8 block of each color. When it is well mixed, flatten the purple clay into a sheet. Then cut a rectangle as tall as your sprocket-hole cane and as wide as you want your pin. This is the backing for the pin. Flatten the remaining purple clay into two sheets, placing one on either side of the sprocket-hole cane.

7. Cut two thin slices from the sprocket-hole cane, and place these on opposite ends of the purple backing. Fill in the space between the sprocket holes with a thin layer of black clay. Create the design in the center using three thin slices from the abstract cane. Cut one slice in half, and arrange all four pieces in the middle section of the pin. Using your fingers or a piece of vellum and a roller, press the slices onto the background.

8. Then turn the pin face down, and position an opened pin back in the center of the pin. Take a tiny ball of black clay, flatten it with your thumb, and press the flattened clay over the center of the pin back until it adheres well to the rest of the clay.

9. Bake the pin at 265°F (130°C) for about 13 to 14 minutes.

10. To make a matching bracelet, cut 11 or more slices (enough to make a bracelet that dangles comfortably around your wrist) from the abstract cane, each about 1/8 inch (3 mm) thick.

11. Pierce each slice through its edges, and bake them all at 265°F (130°C) for about 13 to 14 minutes.

12. Begin one end of your bracelet by looping and crimping the tigertail. String the clay slices alternating with silver beads as shown in the photo; then finish by attaching the clasp to a final loop crimped in place.

Optical Illusions

Materials

(Because it is easier to create a complex design using larger components, a large amount of clay is indicated. If desired, the quantities—and size of your cane—can be reduced proportionally.)

1 block yellow FIMO
5 blocks golden yellow FIMO
1 block carmine FIMO
1 block black FIMO
3 blocks blue FIMO
3 blocks light blue FIMO
3 blocks violet FIMO
3 blocks red FIMO
2 blocks white FIMO
glue
pin back

Tools

rolling tool
slicing blade
craft knife

Instructions

1. In this piece, the gradation of color creates the illusion of three dimensions, adding complexity to a relatively simple design. The star shows four different shades (yellow, yellow-orange, orange, and red-orange), with each color used for two surfaces of the star's points. Mix enough of each shade to make a rectangular log about 1/2 inch (1.3 cm) wide by 1 inch (2.5 cm) high (or whatever size you feel comfortable with, but keep the same proportions). The logs can be as long as you want for your cane.

2. As shown in Figure 1, slice each rectangular log from corner to corner by placing it on its end and slicing down toward your work surface. Then trim off the corners as shown.

3. Combine two sides—one dark and one light—to make each of the star's points. To assemble the star, first combine the points in pairs, then put the two halves together.

4. For the background, make a blue log about the

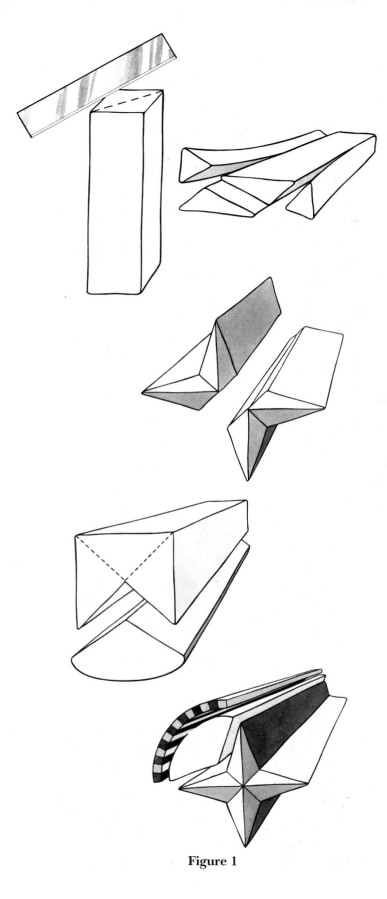

Figure 1

same length as your star cane. Square the log, making it about 1-1/2 inches (3.8 cm) on each side (or proportionally larger or smaller to match your star cane). Then cut the square log from corner to corner in both directions, making four triangular segments.

5. Curve each triangular piece as shown in Figure 1 by carefully pushing down on the center point and rounding out the flat side opposite the point. Repeat with the other triangular pieces.

6. Insert the background pieces between the points of your star, rounding out the cane. To make the design stand out distinctly against the background (as has been done in this example), wrap a paper-thin sheet of black clay completely around the star before adding the background segments. Once the components are all assembled, compact them together and lightly roll the cane. Then set it aside to rest and cool while you assemble the striped patterns for the outside layers.

7. Make two striped loaves to use as your outer coverings. The first is a simple combination of light blue and violet, with alternating colors in multiple thin stripes (see pages 24–25 for more details on making a striped loaf). For the second loaf, place a thin layer of white on each side of a thick sheet of golden yellow, and alternate these "sandwiches" with layers of red.

8. After cutting the star cane into two segments, cut lengthwise slices from each striped loaf to make outer coverings for your canes. Wrap the stripes so they run lengthwise, placing one color combination on one cane segment and the other colors on the second cane.

9. To assemble your pin, first flatten some clay in a complementary color (or black) into a backing sheet about 1/16 inch (about 1.5 mm) thick. Cut slices from your two star canes, making all of the slices the same thickness. To give the design more variety, cut some slices from the star canes after reducing them. Arrange the slices in an abstract pattern, cutting the edges of some to insert others. (This will assure a flat surface on your pin.) To adhere the pieces, press them gently with your fingers, and roll lightly over the top with your roller. Using your craft knife, cut the outline of your design following the edges of your cane slices.

10. Once you're happy with the overall design, bake the piece at 265°F (130°C) for about one hour.

11. After the clay has cooled, attach the pin back with glue.

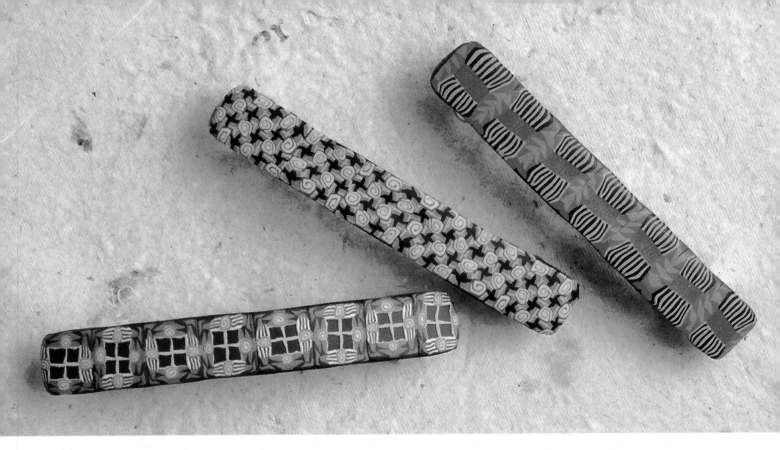

Special-Occasion Barrettes

Materials

pre-constructed cane(s)
small amount of clay in complementary color(s)
barrette back

Tools

slicing blade

Instructions

1. To make a barrette, reduce one of your favorite canes to a diameter slightly larger than the width of your finding. (If you'd like to make one of these patterns, a quick overview of their construction is included below.)

2. Choose or mix some clay in a color that harmonizes with your cane, and make a log somewhat smaller than the barrette finding. When gently flattened onto the top of the metal back, the clay should slightly overextend the hardware on all sides.

3. Using very thin slices, start at one end of the barrette, and position the slices side by side. Gently press the slices onto the backing to blend the seams.

4. With your oven set at the appropriate temperature, bake the clay directly on the barrette for about 15 minutes.

Top Pattern

Begin with alternating stripes of turquoise and navy clay. Slice the cane in half, and insert a wide bar of magenta. Make a second, four-layered, "fish-bone" cane with triangular logs of pink clay as the bones and wedges of blue for the negative space; then place a magenta stripe at top and bottom. Slice the fish-bone cane in half vertically, and apply the right half to the left side of the first cane and the left half to the right side. (When you place slices next to one another, the bones will come together again.)

Center

Start with a magenta and yellow jellyroll that has

been reduced and cut into eight segments; set aside. Using slabs of navy, turquoise, and pink, create a three-layered striped loaf. Cut the cane into four pieces, rotate, and reassemble them so the navy layers form a cross pattern in the center. After reducing this cane to the same diameter as the jellyroll, cut it into eight equal segments. Create the final complex cane by alternating jellyrolls with squares in a checkerboard pattern.

Bottom

Make the center window pane by wrapping a thin sheet of pale peach clay around a black square log. Then reduce the wrapped log, cut it into four equal segments, and reassemble it into a square cane. To make the outer border, start with a jellyroll of bright yellow and medium blue. Reduce the jellyroll, and cut it into four segments. Next make a striped loaf with dark blue and white clay. Cut the loaf into four segments, and pair two segments together horizontally with a jellyroll in the center. Repeat with the second pair. For the second border pattern, use dark blue and pink clay to make a two-layered "fish-bone" cane. Reduce this to a size comparable to the jellyroll; then cut it into four equal segments. Cut each segment of the fish-bone cane in half vertically, making a total of eight half-segments. Place one half-segment on either side of a jellyroll, and finish the pattern by adding a small, flattened log of magenta above the jellyroll. Assemble the border around the window pane, alternating the patterns and using the remaining four half-segments of fish-bone cane as the corner pieces.

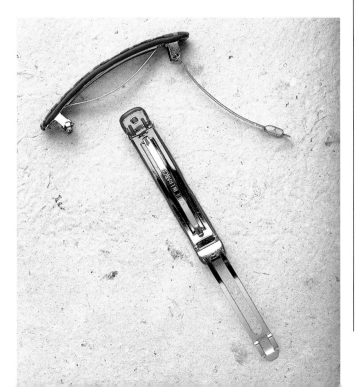

Fanciful Fasteners

Materials

checkerboard: 1/2 block white, 1/2 block black FIMO
rose: 1/2 block green, 1/2 block pink, and 1/4 block red FIMO
swirl: 1/2 block white, 1/2 block light blue, 1/4 block dark blue FIMO
small amount of clay in complementary color(s)
small piece of cardboard or poster board

Tools

rolling tool
slicing blade
craft knife
piercing tool
parchment paper

Instructions

1. Begin by cutting a template from your cardboard, making it whatever size and shape you desire for your buttons. Round ones are easiest—and less likely to fracture if these are functional buttons—but let your imagination be your guide!

2. Then reduce the desired cane(s) to the approximate diameter you want for your buttons (or smaller if your buttons are not circular). A brief summary for constructing the rose and swirl patterns shown here are given below. For instructions on making a checkerboard, see page 27.

3. After flattening your background color into a sheet the thickness you want for your buttons, cut very thin slices from your cane(s), and apply them to the sheet. Press the slices onto the background with your roller.

4. Place the template over the cane slices, and cut out the buttons with a craft knife. Then, with your piercing tool, make two holes in each button.

5. Bake the buttons on oven parchment at 250°F (120°C) for about 30 minutes.

Rose Pattern

After wrapping a pink log with a sheet of red clay, reduce the resulting bull's eye until you can easily cut it into four or five sections. Slice each section in half lengthwise, and arrange the halves into a rose pattern, slightly overlapping them to resemble petals. Fill in the outer openings with small triangular green logs. Then wrap the cane with a sheet of green clay.

Abstract Swirls

For this pattern, flatten one sheet of white, one of
light blue, and two very thin sheets of dark blue.
Sandwich the light blue between the two darker
sheets, and stack it on top of the white one. Flatten
the assembly further; then roll it into a jellyroll.
After slicing the cane lengthwise into pie-shaped
wedges, reassemble the pieces haphazardly to create
an abstract design.

PICTORIAL IMAGERY

Petroglyphs

Materials

1-1/8-inch (2.9 cm) ball of
   black Pro-Mat
blue, red, and gold metallic
   powders
FIMO gloss lacquer
glue
pin back
1 pair earring backs

Tools

rolling tool
craft knife
latex examination gloves
toothpick or other pointed
   object

Instructions

1. Form the clay into a log, and flatten it into a long rectangle about 1/8 inch (3 mm) thick. Using your craft knife, cut one larger rounded rectangle about 2-1/4 by 1-3/8 inches (5.7 by 3.5 cm) for the pin. Then cut two smaller rectangles about 1-1/4 by 1 inch (3.2 by 2.5 cm) for the earrings.

2. Incise your design into the clay with a toothpick, pressing the lines lightly with your finger to smooth the rough edges.

3. Once you have a satisfactory design, enhance it with the metallic powders. For this step it is important to wear gloves and avoid breathing the powder. Dip your gloved finger into the blue metallic powder, and gently rub it on one section of each of your pieces. Using your finger instead of a brush helps keep the powder out of the design lines.

4. Clean your glove, and rub red powder on the other edge of your pieces, leaving a space between the two colors. Now buff the remaining spaces and the outer edges of the pin with the gold powder.

5. Bake all three pieces for 30 minutes at 265°F (130°C).

6. After they have cooled, apply gloss to keep the powders from rubbing off. When the gloss is dry, attach the pin back and earring findings with glue.

A River Runs

Materials

small amounts of orange,
   yellow, dayglow yellow,
   green, blue, white, dayglow
   turquoise, and dayglow
   purple Pro-Mat, all
   totaling 1/4 to 1/2 block
   of clay
pin back
glue
Sculpey or FIMO gloss
   lacquer

Tools

rolling tool
craft knife
wooden clay tool
pencil or other dull
   pointed tool
jeweler's wax-working tool
   or fountain pen nib
parchment paper
medium sandpaper
small paintbrush

Instructions

1. Begin by mixing your colors. This piece treats the polymer clay as if it were paint—add a dab of this and that to get just the tones you like. For example, the outer frame is a combination of orange and white, and the yellow river is created from equal amounts of yellow and dayglow yellow mixed together with a small amount of white. As you can see by the photograph, many of the colors merge and blend, evolving from dark to light. Experiment with several color combinations until you find those you like best.

2. To make the frame, use a photocopy of the pattern shown here, or let your imagination guide your hand. Flatten the pale orange clay into a sheet about 1/8 inch (3 mm) thick. Then, with the pattern placed on top, use a craft knife to cut the inner and outer borders of the frame.

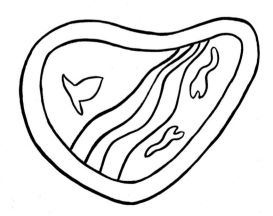

Figure 1

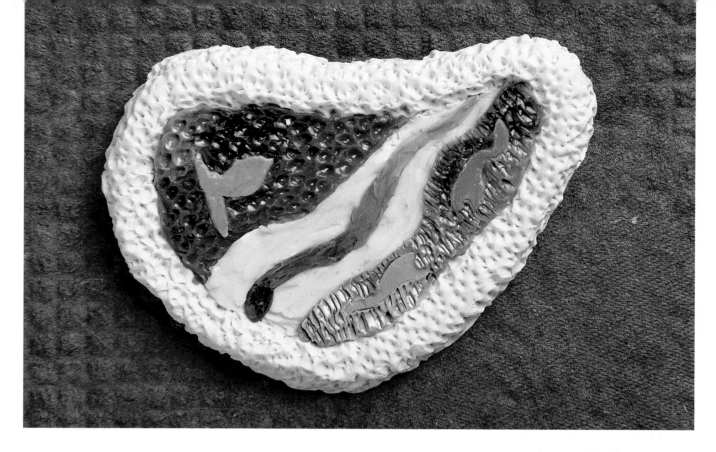

3. Next flatten a piece of blue clay to the same thickness. This is your backing, and creating an exact color shade is not essential. Place the light orange frame on top of the blue sheet, and cut around the outside of the frame to shape the backing. Remove any excess clay. Using the wooden tool, push the frame down around the outside of the blue clay, totally covering the blue edges with a rounded frame. In addition, press the frame down around the inside to make the two colors adhere completely. Using the tip of a pencil, make dotted indentations into the frame.

4. Now cut your animal shapes—two snakes and a fish—from small, thin (about 1/32 inch or .8 mm) sheets of clay.

5. Bake the backing with its frame and the separate animals on a piece of oven parchment, setting your oven at 275°F (135°C). Remove the animals after about 10 minutes; leave the frame in for a total of 20 minutes.

6. While the other pieces are cooling, prepare the purple, blue, blue-black, dark and light green, dark and light blue-green, and pale yellow clays. Mix these until you have tones and combinations of tones that look pleasing.

7. After flattening the yellow clay into a sheet about 1/16 inch (1.6 mm) thick, cut the river pieces that run diagonally across the pin. With the jeweler's tool or pen nib, roughen the surface of the backing piece; then set the river pieces onto the backing, gently pressing them o stick to the backing.

8. Using small pieces of clay, fill in the rest of the background colors, blending them together with the jeweler's tool. Use at least three different tones of green and blue-green to make the green pattern in the middle of the river. Once the background colors are blended to your liking, take the hardened animal pieces and carefully press them into their correct positions on the piece. Use the tip of the jeweler's tool to make the pattern on the dark colors at the top of the piece. With the side of the tool, make the grass pattern at the bottom. Then smooth the yellow and green clay in the river.

9. Bake the finished piece at 275°F (135°C) for about 20 minutes.

10. After it has cooled, rub the back of the piece with medium sandpaper. Then glue on the pin back.

11. For a final touch, use a small paintbrush to apply gloss lacquer to the background but not to the river or the animals.

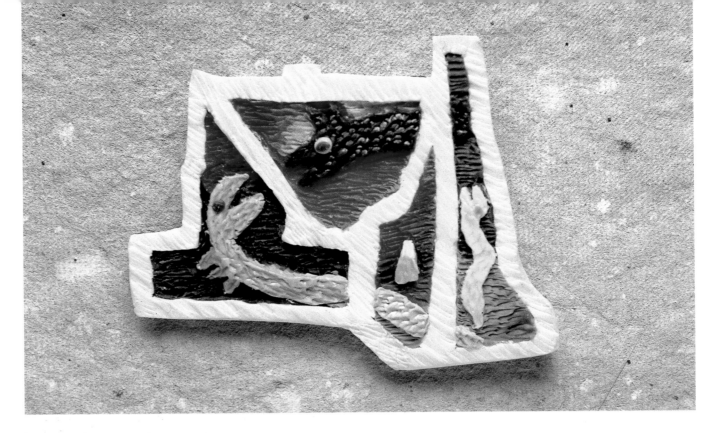

Dangerous Pets

Materials

small amounts of pearlescent
white, black, blue,
turquoise, red, purple,
green, yellow, and dayglow
yellow Pro-Mat, all
totaling about 1/4 to 1/2
block of clay
glue
pin back
Sculpey or FIMO lacquer

Tools

rolling tool
craft knife
jeweler's wax-working tool
or fountain pen nib
parchment paper
sandpaper
small paintbrush

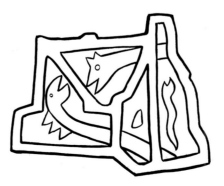

Figure 1

Instructions

1. Using a photocopy machine, make a copy of
   Figure 1 to use as a template. Place the pattern
   onto a sheet of white clay flattened to a thickness of about 1/16 inch (1.6 mm). With your
   craft knife, cut through the paper to mark the
   outlines of the frame on the clay, starting from
   the inside and working toward the outside
   edges. Then remove the paper, and cut through
   the clay with the craft knife. Set aside the extra-
   neous pieces.

2. After flattening the black clay into a sheet 1/8 inch (3 mm) thick, set the white frame on top of the black sheet. Cut around the outside of the white frame through the black clay underneath, and remove any excess clay.

3. Press the two together and, using the side of the jeweler's tool or pen nib, make a line pattern on the white frame. With the tool or your fingers, smooth the edges all around.

4. Bake this piece at 275°F (135°C) for about 20 minutes.

5. After the piece has cooled, roughen the inside (black) sections with sandpaper.

6. For the background colors, mix a deep blue-black, a dark, blackened turquoise, several tones of red, a few of purple, and a bright, light green. Using small bits of clay, fill in the appropriate spaces within the frame. Place a few similar tones in close proximity to each other, and blend the edges with your jeweler's tool. Then make the linear pattern in the background using the same tool. Your goal is to have subtle gradations; if you're not happy with the results, just peel off the unbaked clay and try again.

7. For the animals, you'll need light blue (equal parts of white and blue), light yellow (a small amount of white mixed with equal portions of yellow and dayglow yellow), and black. Form each animal from tiny logs of clay, making sure to continue its body from one room of the "house" to another. Use the tool to manipulate the clay into the desired shapes and to incise the surface patterns onto the animals. To make the eyes, form tiny balls of clay. For the miniature volcano, blend some white clay with a minuscule amount of orange and purple to make a light brown.

8. When the design is complete, place the pin on a sheet of oven parchment, and bake it at 275°F (135°C) for 20 minutes.

9. After the piece has cooled, lightly sand the back surface, and attach the finding with glue.

10. With a small paintbrush, apply lacquer to each of the animals.

Jungle Scene

Materials

1/4 block white polymer clay (any brand will work, but it must be freshly opened)
piece of clean, white paper
small amounts of medium green, light green, and violet clay
piece of vellum or wax paper
pin back
glue

Tools

rolling tool
craft knife
burnisher or dull, flat instrument

Instructions

1. Choose any copyright-free image from gift wrapping paper, note cards, or the jungle fabric reproduced here. Using a color copier, reduce the image to fit within the T-shirt outline for this pin. If you use this jungle scene, copy the image at 50%. Other images may need to be reduced to 50% or smaller to use for jewelry. Any color copier will work; just make sure that the toner in the machine is fresh.

2. Flatten the white clay into a sheet approximately 1/4 inch (6 mm) thick. To remove the excess oils, lay a piece of clean, white paper on top of the clay, leaving it in place at least overnight.

3. Using the outline in Figure 1, cut through the clay to make a T-shirt shape.

4. After trimming your color copy to roughly the same size as your sheet of clay, lay the image face down onto the clay. To assist the transfer process, gently rub the entire surface with a

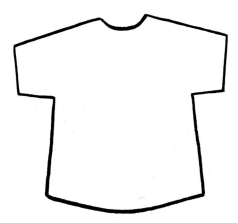

Figure 1

burnisher or other dull instrument. The key
term is gently; don't press too hard.

5. Allow the copy to rest undisturbed on the clay for
   15 to 30 minutes. You can lift a corner of the copy
   to determine if the image has transferred success-
   fully. The process may need more time, but probably no more than an hour total. When you are satisfied with the image, remove the paper. If you
   leave the image on too long, it may stick to the
   clay or blur the transfer. To remove paper that has
   gotten stuck, moisten a cotton swab with some fingernail polish remover, and gently rub the paper.
   Be sure to do this in a well-ventilated room.

6. You may decide to leave your image as is. If you
   prefer to embellish it, form some violet and
   green clay into triangular-shaped logs. Cut thin
   slices from all three colors, and apply them
   around the edges of the pin and wherever else
   your eye tells you they're needed. Lay the vellum or wax paper on top and, using a roller,
   press the slices into the image. Be careful not
   to touch the image with your fingers, or it
   might smear.

7. Following the manufacturer's guidelines, bake
   your pin.

8. When cooled, glue the pin back in place.

Taking Flight

Materials

*1/4 block white polymer clay
(any brand will work for a
photo-transfer, but use
fresh, not leftover material)
piece of clean, white paper
colored pencils (Prismacolor
pencils work nicely)
red, black, and blue permanent markers
1/4 block of black or other
color clay for backing
small amounts of several
colors of clay
small piece of metallic leaf
pin back
glue*

Tools

*rolling tool
burnisher or dull, flat
instrument
craft knife*

Instructions

1. Select the image you want to reproduce for your pin. If you choose the crane pictured here, set the color copier to 62%. Otherwise, reduce your image sufficiently to fit inside your pin outline. To get the best possible transfer, make sure the copier has fresh toner when you use it.

2. Using white material fresh from the package (not leftovers that have been handled frequently), flatten the clay into a sheet approximately 1/8 inch (3 mm) thick. Remove any excess oils by laying a piece of clean, white paper on top of the clay and leaving it in place overnight.

3. Use the outlines of the pin shape in Figure 1 to make two templates, one smaller and one larger. Place the smaller template on the white sheet, and cut the clay with your craft knife.

4. To make a backing for your piece, flatten a second sheet of clay about 1/8 inch (3 mm) thick. Choose a color that goes well with your image,

103

6. After allowing the copy to rest undisturbed on the clay for 15 to 30 minutes, lift one corner to see if the image has transferred. The process may need more time, but don't let it sit too long, or the image may blur or the paper stick.

7. This image is rather pale when transferred. To give it some "punch," darken specific places—wings, neck, eye, background—with colored pencils and fine-point permanent markers. While you're working, try to avoid smudging the image with your fingers.

8. Now make the decorative border. This consists of a number of cane slices, all about 1/8 inch (3 mm) thick, applied around the edges of the image. Build several striped loaves using a mixture of colors that go well with your image. This pin includes: magenta, lilac, light blue, violet, orange, green, ochre, fluorescent pink, white, black, and black with metallic leaf.

9. Once you have the slices arranged to your liking, press them gently in place onto the backing. Then trim off any excess around the edges.

10. Bake the pin according to the manufacturer's guidelines, but check it periodically to make sure the clay doesn't darken.

11. When the piece has cooled, glue the finding in place.

or use everyone's favorite standby—black. Then use the larger template to cut the backing. With the white layer centered onto the backing, compress the two together, rolling them gently to squeeze out any air bubbles.

5. Trim your color copy to match the size of the white clay zigzag, and lay the image face down onto the clay. Then gently rub the entire surface with a burnisher, a dull letter opener or other similar instrument. This helps transfer the image.

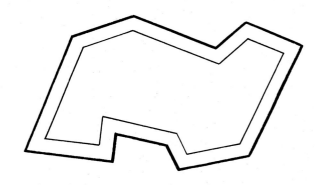

Figure 1

PURE TEXTURE

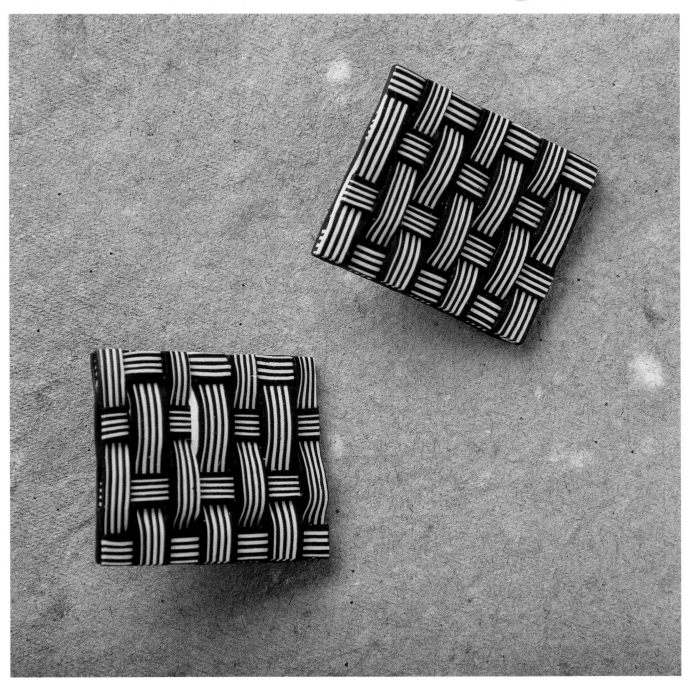

Classic Weave

Materials

1 block white FIMO
1 block black FIMO
2 earring backs
glue

Tools

rolling tool
craft knife
slicing blade
wax paper
toothpick or knitting
  needle

Instructions

1. Divide each block of clay into four equal balls, and flatten each one into a sheet about 2-1/4 by 5 inches (5.7 by 12.7 cm). Measure and trim each sheet, or use a template as a guide to cut your clay sheets.

2. Setting the first layer on a piece of wax paper, stack all eight sheets together, alternating colors.

3. After gently compressing the layers together with your fingers and roller, cut the rectangular loaf in half. Turn one piece upside-down, and place it on top of the other half to continue the striped pattern. Now reduce the square loaf by squeezing and gently stretching it until you have at least doubled the length. (You will need long, thin pieces for weaving.) You may want to cut a trial slice across the shorter end to check the width of your stripes. Don't compress the cane so much that the pattern is lost altogether.

4. When the cane is to your liking, trim the edges all around. If you're using a wallpaper scraping blade or tissue slicing blade, you may want to cut the cane to the length of your blade. It is easier to make the weavers a consistent thickness if you press the full length of the blade down through the clay in one motion.

5. To make the strips for weaving, cut thin slices lengthwise from the loaf. Lay each slice—stripes facing up—on a piece of wax paper. The strips should lie parallel, touching each other. You can use them as is or, for the more delicate weave shown here, you can cut each in half lengthwise before starting to weave. Add slices until you have twice the length you want for each earring. (You weave both together, and cut them apart later.) In hand weaving or basketry terms, this is your warp.

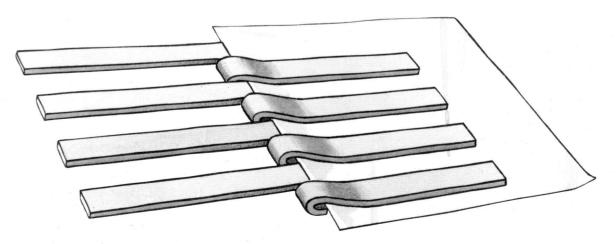

Figure 1

6. Press the side of your thumb along the top edge of your slices, just enough so the strips won't separate from the wax paper when you manipulate them. Now place another piece of wax paper (about the size of your weaving square) at the top of the square, overlapping the clay by about 3/8 inch (1 cm). You'll use this to prevent the individual strips from sticking to your weaving as it progresses.

7. Starting at the right edge of your warp, carefully lift the first slice and flip it over, guiding it back out of the way (see Figure 1). Maintain the curve in your slice; don't press it down onto the wax paper. Skip the next slice, and lift up the third strip. Continue lifting alternating strips until you reach the full width of your warp.

8. For your weft, cut about eight additional slices from your loaf, and set these aside on another piece of wax paper. If you cut the first ones in half lengthwise, do the same with these. Lay one of the weft slices across the width of the warp close to the top where you've adhered the grouping to the wax paper.

9. Now, moving from right to left, lower each raised strip, and raise each lowered one. Then lay your next weft piece across. Adjust the spacing of the slices as you work to make sure it looks even all across the weaving, and gradually draw the wax paper down to protect the finished weaving. Continue the process until you are at the bottom of your weaving.

10. Using scraps from making your loaf, or other matching clay, make a ball, and flatten it into a sheet equal in size to your weaving. This backing layer should also be about the same thickness as your weaving.

11. Pick up your weaving, turn it face down in your hand, and remove the wax paper. Then place the weaving face up onto the backing sheet.

12. Now cut the piece in half, and trim the edges to make two matching earrings. Try to trim each earring right at the edges of your strips. Then lightly pinch the edges of the weaving and the backing together to make them adhere completely. Smooth out any rough places with a toothpick or knitting needle.

13. Bake the earrings at 250°F (120°C) for 20 to 30 minutes.

14. When they're cool, glue the findings in place.

Textured Swirls

Materials

1/2 block purple Sculpey III
gold buffing compound
clear lacquer finish
glue
2 earring backs

Tools

screen, basket, fabric, or
    other textured surface
rolling tool

Instructions

1. Divide the clay in half, and roll each half into a log about 9 inches (22.9 cm) long. Then bend each log into a swirl, making one portion overlap the other.

2. Lay both swirls onto a piece of screen or other textured surface, and use your roller to flatten the logs and impress the texture onto the clay.

3. Once you have an interesting pattern, bake the earrings at 225°F (107°C) for about 40 minutes.

4. When the earrings have cooled, rub on the gold buffing compound, and apply the clear lacquer finish. Use glue to attach the earring backs.

Corporate Counter Culture

Materials

2–3 blocks clay for base color
  of tie
1/4 block each of three
  different colors for pattern
graph paper (optional)
wax paper
1-1/2 yards (1.4 m)
  grosgrain ribbon or chain
2 earring backs
glue

Tools

rolling tool
craft knife
slicing blade

Instructions

1. Enlarge the necktie and knot patterns with a photocopier (set at 125%), or draw them onto graph paper, making any adjustment you like. Then cut out the pattern templates.

2. Making sure your clay is well conditioned, flatten the background color into slabs large enough to accommodate the tie and knot patterns. For stability, the slabs should be between 1/8 and 1/4 inch (3 to 6 mm) thick.

3. Now trace the outline of the two patterns onto the clay with your craft knife. (Don't actually cut the clay; it's easier if you wait until after applying the designs.)

4. If you haven't already made some patterned canes that you'd like to use, make one or more now. Stripes and dots are old favorites, or use your imagination to make simple or elaborate combinations of millefiore designs. Be creative! A handsome example is shown in the photo on the following page: a combination of abstract patterns and bull's eyes in black, white, tan, and red is displayed on a taupe background.

5. Using your slicing blade, cut very thin slices of your cane, and arrange the pattern pieces inside the necktie and knot outlines on your background sheets. Once you have them arranged the way you want them, place a piece of wax paper on top of the clay. With your roller, press the wax paper to smooth the patterns into the clay.

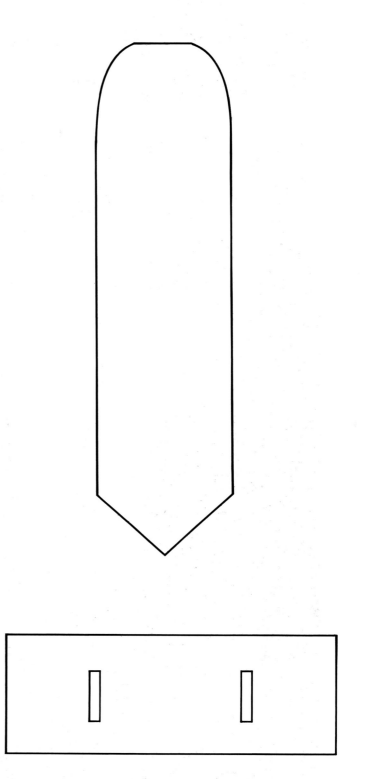

Figure 1

6. When you remove the wax paper, you may find that your original outlines have faded. If so, retrace them. Then, using a craft knife, cut out the necktie and knot. After cutting out the knot, round off the top corners. Now cut slits into the knot to accommodate your ribbon or chain.

7. To make the necktie look realistic, pinch and adjust the top, giving it a three-dimensional curve. Center the knot at the top of the necktie, and pinch the tie and knot together. Now carefully fold the knot around the necktie, overlapping the two ends of the knot at the back. The slits should be unobtrusive on the sides.

8. Following the manufacturer's recommendations for the brand of clay you're using, bake your tie.

9. Allow the necktie to cool completely before removing it from your baking surface. Then string the chain or ribbon through the slits. To keep the tie centered on your ribbon, insert the ribbon through the first slit, tie a knot, then insert the ribbon through the second slit.

10. The matching earrings shown in the photo are made with scraps of the background clay flattened into a sheet. Apply several additional cane slices to the sheet, and cut two squares or other shapes for earrings. Bake them with the tie, and attach the findings with glue.

One Perfect Rose

Materials

1/4 block pink pearl Sculpey III

1/4 block metallic green Sculpey III

small amounts of pearl and black Sculpey III

metallic paints: Deco Art Glorious Gold and Ebony Black

pin back

glue

Tools

rolling tool

craft knife

crochet hook, knitting needle, or anything else of similar shape

toothpicks

small, stiff-bristled brush

liner brush

Instructions

1. With the multitude of colors available, your rose pin can be made to match any color scheme. For a realistic flower, choose a soft pink for the petals, and mix a dull, gray-green for the leaves. (You can dull the bright green by adding small amounts of pearl and black.)

2. Pinch off enough leaf-colored clay to make a ball about 2 inches (5 cm) in diameter. Flatten this into a sheet about 1/16 inch (1.6 mm) thick. Using the pattern in Figure 1 as your guide, cut out one leaf. Score the veins into the leaf with your craft knife, and use the back of the crochet hook or knitting needle to create the notched leaf edges. Repeat this procedure until you have completed three leaves.

3. Arrange the three leaves in a triangular pattern with their bases pressed together to form a foundation for the pin. To avoid damaging the shape later, it is advisable to arrange the leaves directly on the surface you plan to use for baking.

4. Take a small amount of petal-colored clay, and roll it into a ball about 1/4 inch (6 mm) in diameter. Flatten this between your thumb and index finger to create a rectangular shape about 1/16 inch (1.6 mm) thick. (Slight variations in thickness make the rose look more realistic.) Starting at one end, roll the sheet downward at a slight angle to make a tight bud. Roll three additional 1/4-inch (6 mm) balls of clay, and press these into ovals about 1/16 inch (1.6 mm)

thick. Wrap the three petals, one at a time, around the bud, making sure to stagger and overlap them slightly. You now have a complete rosebud. (See the photo above.)

5. For a fully opened rose, roll five additional balls, each about 1/2 inch (1.3 cm) in diameter. Press these into ovals 1/16 inch (1.6 mm) thick, and wrap them around the rose bud. After curling each petal outward slightly, roll the base of the rose gently between your thumb and index finger to secure the petals together. Then cut off any excess clay at the base of the flower to make it flat.

6. Insert a toothpick at a slight angle directly into the center of the rosebud, being careful not to put it all the way through the rose. Lift the rose, and place it in the center of the three leaves. After pressing the rose gently onto the leaves, carefully remove the toothpick by twisting it slightly and lifting it out slowly. Gently lift, twist, and curl the points of the leaves to give them a natural shape.

7. Bake the pin at 275°F (135°C) for about 15 minutes.

8. After the pin has cooled thoroughly, glue on the finding.

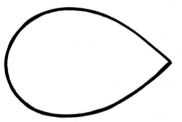

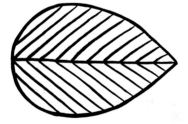

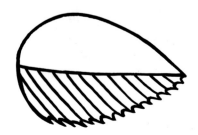

Figure 1

Fortune's Amulet

Materials

3 blocks transparent FIMO
1/4 block turquoise FIMO
1/8 block white FIMO
variegated composition
   metallic leaf
white acrylic paint
a few miscellaneous beads
   and spacers from old
   jewelry (optional)
white round elastic
glue

Tools

rolling tool
slicing blade
modelling tool
1/2-inch (1.3 cm) diameter
   hole cutter (copper tubing
   works well)
metal skewer or coat hanger
darning needle

Instructions

1. To construct the complex cane used for this
   bracelet, you'll make four sets of components
   and two interim canes. Make all of the square
   component sheets about the same size, and trim
   the canes so they are equal in length to the
   sheets. For the #1 components, mix 1/2 block of
   transparent clay with less than 1/8 block
   turquoise. Reserve a 1/2- to 3/4-inch (1.3 to 1.9
   cm) ball for the next step, and flatten the balance into a square sheet about 1/8 inch (3 mm)
   thick. Then cut the sheet into quarters.

2. For the #2 components, mix 1/2 block transparent with the reserved ball of clay from step 1.
   Flatten this into a sheet about half as thick as in
   step 1. Then cut four pieces about the same size
   as the #1 components. Reserve the remainder of
   the combination for later.

3. Using 1/4 block of transparent clay, make two
   more identical square sheets. Form another
   1/4 block of transparent clay into a log. Then
   cut the log into four components each as long

as the square sheets. All of these are #3 components.

4. Flatten 1/4 block of transparent clay into a sheet about 1/4 inch (3 mm) thick, and place a piece of metallic leaf on top. Using your roller, press the leaf onto the clay. Continue to roll, stretching the clay and cracking the leaf. If you have problems with the clay sticking to the work surface, use your fingers to do some of the stretching. When the sheet is more than twice the size of your component squares, cut off a strip about 1 inch (2.5 cm) wide to make component #4, and set the strip aside until you make the beads. Using the remainder of the sheet, cut four pieces, and stack these into a cane. Cut the cane in half, stack the components, cut in half, and stack again. Reduce the height of the finished cane (Cane A) to about 1/2 inch (1.3 cm), and trim it to the length of the square sheets made previously (components 1-3). Reserve any trimmings.

5. Make a second interim cane—Cane B—using 1/4 block of transparent mixed with less than 1/16 block of white. Flatten the clay into a sheet about 1/8 inch (3 mm) thick, and cut it in half. Using one piece, cut two squares the same size as all the previous ones. Flatten the other half until it is large enough to make four more identical squares. Using the balance of the light turquoise clay from step 2, flatten a sheet, and cut six more identical squares. Now build a cane alternating thick and thin sheets of the pale white clay with the light turquoise layers. Cut

the cane in half, stack the pieces, and reduce the thickness of the cane. Do this at least twice. Make the final cane the same height as Cane A and about twice as wide.

6. The final, working cane might be considered a hoagie sandwich (or hero or grinder, depending on your geography) because of the number of layers. If you start to get confused, refer to Figure 1. Otherwise, here goes from the bottom up:

Start with component #3	Lay one square sheet on a clean working surface. Then place two of the #3 logs on the sheet.
Add #2 layer.	
Add #1 layer.	
Add #2 layer.	
Add Cane B.	Cut the cane into eight lengthwise slices, each about 1/8 inch (3 mm) thick. Place four of the slices horizontally on top of the #2 layer. (The stripes will be vertical.)
Add #2 layer	
Add Cane B.	Place the remaining four slices so the stripes are vertical.
Add the last #2 layer.	
Add #1 layer.	
Add #3 layer	Stretch the remaining square until it is twice as long as it was. Cut it in half, and place one half on top of the #1 layer.

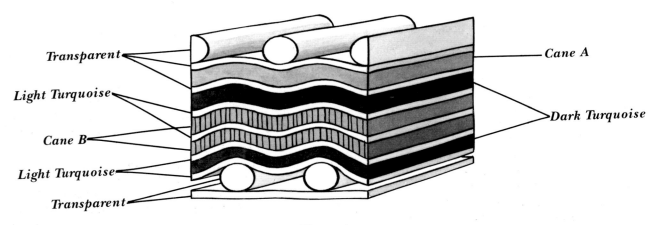

Transparent

Light Turquoise

Cane B

Light Turquoise

Transparent

Cane A

Dark Turquoise

Figure 1

heavy piece of wire, make an indentation in the top to hold the "jewel." This is a small dot of transparent clay inserted into the indentation.

8. For the hourglass beads, use additional transparent clay to make three logs. Vary the sizes slightly from 1/4 to 3/8 inch (6 mm to 1 cm) in diameter and from 1 to 1-1/4 inch (2.5 to 3 cm) long. Cut thin slices from the hoagie cane, and wrap them completely around the transparent logs as if you were making bull's eyes. Then cut 1/2-inch (1.3 cm) circles from the reserved strip of combination #4. Use these to cap the ends of two or more of the wrapped logs. Roll the capped ends lightly on your work surface to compress the clay and slightly round the ends. Now form each bead into an hourglass shape by gently rolling it in the center.

9. Make several round beads from your scrap materials. Three should be about 1/2 inch (1.3 cm) in diameter, and six or more smaller ones can vary from flat disks to small balls. Make all of the beads large enough to accommodate a skewer-sized hole. This allows insertion of the elastic later. Wrap one of the beads with some of the metallic leaf (combination #4). Make another into a doughnut shape.

10. To make the cone-shaped bead, start with a 1/2-inch (1.3 cm) ball of trimmings from Cane A. Shape it into a cone, and cap the large end with a circle of the combination #4 metallic leaf.

11. The final bead is actually a shark vertebra inlaid with scraps of clay. You can create something very similar by making a disk 5/8 inch (1.6 cm) in diameter and 1/4 inch (6 mm) thick. Press the sides in to make them concave, and carve out indentations around the edge.

12. Pierce all of the beads, including the scarab, with the skewer. Make the hole in one of the round beads large enough to hold the knot you will tie in the elastic.

13. Bake all of the beads at 240°F (115°C) for about 30 minutes.

14. To antique the scarab, brush it with white acrylic paint. Before it can dry, immediately wipe the paint from the surface, leaving it in the incised areas. For a smooth sheen, buff the surface with a bit of wax on a soft cloth.

15. Assemble the beads on the elastic, beginning with the round bead with the larger hole. Adjust the length to fit your wrist, and tie the elastic with an overhand knot hidden inside the bead. A drop of glue on the knot is added insurance.

Add Cane "A."	Slice the cane into four lengthwise segments each about 1/8 inch (3 mm) thick. Lay the slices horizontally across the #3 layer so that the stripes of gold flecks are vertical.
Add #3 layer.	Place the remaining half-sheet over the cane. then lay one #3 log down the center of the cane, and slice the remaining log in half lengthwise, placing the two halves at the edges as shown in Figure 1.

Congratulations! Your hoagie is complete. Now compress it first with your hands, then with a roller to make it approximately 1-3/4 inches (4.4 cm) wide by 1-1/2 inches (3.8 cm) high.

7. To make the scarab, mix a 1/2- to 3/4-inch (1.3 to 1.9 cm) ball of turquoise clay with a small, pea-sized ball of white. Form this into an oval bead that is flat on one side, modelling it to look like a scarab. Use the modelling tool to incise the scarab markings. With your skewer or a

Community Gathering

Materials

1 block anthracite FIMO
metallic buffing compounds:
  Rub'n Buff Spanish
  copper, silver leaf, and
  antique gold
matte or semi-matte lacquer
  finish
1 yard (91 cm) leather cord

Tools

2 needle tools, one sharp
  and one very blunt
  (see below)
#1 and #2 paintbrushes
small shell
pieces of fabric
parchment paper

Instructions

1. Following the guidelines on pages 31–32, sculpt three faces about 3/4 inch (1.9 cm) high. Add character lines around the eyes and mouth of each face, and make each one slightly different in expression.

2. To make the hanger for the pendant, roll a 5/8-inch (1.6 cm) ball of clay into a strip about 1-1/2 inch (3.8 cm) long and 1/8 inch (3 mm) thick. Softly fold the strip in half, pressing the ends together. Leave a hole in the center large enough to accommodate the leather cord.

3. For the backing, flatten a 3/4-inch (1.9 cm) ball of clay into a circle about 1-3/4 inch (4.4 cm) in diameter. Press the circular backing onto the base of the hanger, over the hanger ends. Then lay the construction onto a piece of oven parchment.

4. Begin the draping by pressing a strip of clay about 1-3/4 by 3/4 inch (4.4 by 1.9 cm) onto the bottom right of the backing circle. Place one head on top of the strip, and curl the strip softly around the face, curling each end into a soft roll.

5. To create textured hair, press small, flat strips of clay against the rough surface of a shell or other corrugated object. If the clay tends to stick, try coating the shell with a light dusting of talcum powder or water (not both). Press the hair along the side of the face not already draped.

6. Flatten a strip of clay about 2 inches (5 cm) long, pressing it against a piece of fabric to create an interesting texture. Then wrap the sheet 1-1/2 times around a second face, and place this face to the left of the first one. Using your fingers, curl the edges of the drape back, away from the face. Don't let any thin edges protrude where they might catch on your clothing and break.

7. Now press a third face above the other two. Flatten another 2-inch (5 cm) strip of clay, and drape it over the head. Bring the ends of the draping down onto the adjacent figures to tie the three together. Form a curl at one end and a loose curve at the other.

8. For the final draping, flatten a larger strip about 5 by 3/4 inches (12.7 by 1.9 cm). Add texture by pressing one portion against a shell and the other section against a piece of fabric. Then drape this strip around the top and sides of the total piece. Turn the edges of the strip to the back, pressing them firmly so that all of the pieces join together. Check the back of the piece to see if all unsightly edges are covered. If not, carefully add small strips of clay to cover any gaps.

9. Bake the pendant at 265°F (130°C) for 30 minutes.

10. After baking, brush on the metallic rubbing compounds. The colors can be thinned with mineral spirits and blended to create muted shades. After the metallic finish has dried thoroughly, apply the matte or semi-matte sealer.

11. Slip your pendant onto the leather cord, tie a knot, and your necklace is complete.

Nautilus

Materials

1/4 block bronze Sculpey III
1/8 block metallic purple
  Sculpey III
1/8 block pewter Sculpey III
1/8 block metallic green
  Sculpey III
1/8 block metallic blue
  Sculpey III
small amount turquoise Pro-
  Mat
1 - 4 mm fluted brass bead
2 - 2 mm fluted brass beads
14 - 3 mm bugle beads in iri-
  descent colors
short lengths of 20-gauge
  niobium wire, 20-gauge
  brass wire, and 18-gauge
  sterling silver wire
1 - 3 mm blue glass bead
gloss lacquer
glue
pin back
1 pair earring backs

Tools

needle-nose pliers
sandpaper

Instructions

1. Begin by mixing your colors. Make wine by combining 1/16 block each of bronze and metallic
   purple. For mauve, add 1/32 block of pewter to
   an equal amount of metallic purple. Olive
   results from mixing 1/16 block each of bronze
   and metallic green. Add 1/16 block of pewter
   to 1/16 block metallic blue to get blue-gray.

2. Roll the mauve clay into a log about 4-1/2 to
   5 inches (11.4 to 12.7 cm) long, and roll the
   wine clay into a log twice that long. Cut the
   wine log in half lengthwise, and sandwich the
   mauve log, forming a three-striped band.
   Flatten the band, pulling it slightly until it is
   about 1/8 inch (3 mm) thick and as wide as
   the crescent patterns in Figure 1. Curve the
   band to fit the patterns, cut the lengths
   indicated, and set the pieces aside.

3. Now roll the olive clay into a log about 7 inches
   (17.8 cm) long with one end slightly pointed.
   After making a second, similar log using the
   blue-gray clay, lay the two side by side with the
   pointed ends together. Beginning at the pointed
   ends, slowly roll the two logs together jellyroll
   fashion. Flatten, pressing the edges together, to

Figure 1

Figure 2

6. To make the striped cylinders, start with about 1/32 block of these colors: metallic green, metallic blue, metallic purple, and bronze. Roll each piece into a log about 4 inches (10.2 cm) long. Twist the four together, pulling as you twist. Cut pieces to match the length and diameter of the patterns. To prevent excess flattening when you apply them to the pin and earrings, place the short candy canes into the freezer for five or ten minutes. Then, using the photo as a guide for placement, attach the striped canes onto the jewelry pieces.

7. Bake all three pieces at 265°F (130°C) for about 30 minutes.

8. While the pieces are baking, cut a 3-1/4-inch (8.3 cm) length of niobium wire, and roll one end into a tight spiral. Using smooth needle-nose pliers, shape the end into a small hook. (The hook prevents the wire from sliding out of the finished piece.) Cut a 1-3/4-inch (4.4 cm) length of brass wire, curving it into an abstract shape with a glass bead placed in the center. Using the smooth pliers, flatten one end of a 1-5/8-inch (4.1 cm) length of silver wire, and shape the wire into a zigzag. The wire forms are shown in Figure 2.

9. After the pin has baked and cooled, turn it over, and sand the lower spiral area. Make a 1/2-inch (1.3 cm) ball of turquoise Pro-Mat, and press it firmly onto the sanded part of the pin. Manipulate the clay into a kidney shape, and slide the three wires into the soft clay. Press the clay around the wires and smooth it, making sure the turquoise does not show from the front.

10. Bake the pin again at 265°F (130°C) for about 25 minutes.

11. When the pin has cooled, apply gloss lacquer if desired, and glue on the findings.

a thickness of about 1/8 inch (3 mm). Continue rolling and flattening until the spiral is the size of the pattern for the pin. Then cut the ends at a 45-degree angle so that the edges are smooth with the rest of the spiral.

4. Slowly and evenly pull the remaining log combination until it is almost twice as long as the original. Bending the blue-gray point down over the olive, begin a smaller spiral. Flatten as you roll, and continue until this spiral is the size of the earring pattern. Cut the ends, and repeat for the second earring.

5. Assemble the pin and earrings on your baking sheet by overlapping the spirals on top of the crescents. Now press the brass beads into the middle of the spirals, using the larger one on the pin. Scatter several bugle beads on the crescents, pressing them firmly to embed them into the clay.

Autumn Leaves

Materials

1 block metallic copper
  Sculpey III
1 block metallic green
  Sculpey III
Deco Art Dazzling Metallics
  acrylic paints: Royal Ruby
  and Glorious Gold
paper towels
42 black glass seed beads
monofilament or tigertail
  jewelry wire
2 crimp beads
clasp
1 pair earring backs

Tools

rolling tool
craft knife
bamboo skewer
crochet hook, knitting
  needle or other similar
  object
piercing tool
small, stiff-bristled
  paintbrush

Instructions

1. Begin by blending the two colors of clay just
   enough to marbleize them. This combination of
   warm and cool tones reflects the woodlands
   inspiration for the piece, but you could easily
   substitute others.

2. Flatten one piece of the mixed clay into a sheet
   about 1/8 inch (3 mm) thick. Then cut the
   sheet into a rectangle 3 inches (7.6 cm) long
   by 1 inch (2.5 cm) wide. Placing the wooden
   skewer in the center, fold the sheet in half
   lengthwise. Gently press the long edges together, and carefully twist the skewer to prevent the
   clay from sticking to it. This makes the foundation for the leaves.

3. To create the leaves for the necklace, flatten a
   sheet of the mixed clay to a thickness of about
   1/8 inch (3 mm). Using the pattern in Figure 1
   (enlarged at 122%), cut seven leaves, lightly
   scoring each with a knife where veining is indicated. Place leaves #1 and #2 at slight angles on
   each end of the foundation as shown in Figure
   2. Add the remaining leaves in order as indicated. Once you have a pleasing arrangement,
   press all of the leaves gently to adhere them to
   the foundation. As noted in the figure, curl several of the leaf edges with your fingers to make
   them look natural, not stiff and flat.

4. For the acorns, use some brown clay to make a
   ball about 3/8 inch (1 cm) in diameter. With
   your fingers, shape the bottom into a gentle
   point resembling an acorn, and flatten the top.

Lightly stroke the surface with the back of a crochet hook or knitting needle to make vertical grooves. Roll a second 3/8-inch (1 cm) ball of brown clay, and flatten it between your thumb and forefinger to a thickness of about 1/8 inch (3 mm). Shape this into a cap for the top of your acorn. Again using the crochet hook or other tool, lightly press dimples into the cap. Repeat this process until you have completed the desired number of acorns. Position them randomly on the leaves, pressing them just enough to adhere the clay.

5. To make matching earrings, flatten a sheet of the mixed clay to a thickness of about 1/8 inch (3 mm). Using Figure 3 enlarged at 122%, cut one right and one left leaf, scoring the veins and curling the edges as indicated.

6. Bake the earrings and the pectoral piece at 275°F (135°C) for about 15 minutes.

7. While these pieces are baking, begin making the round beads. You'll need 42 in total: 34 beads about 5/16 inch (8 mm) in diameter, and eight beads about 3/8 inch (1 cm) in diameter. The process moves more quickly if you make a long log and cut even segments to roll into balls.

8. Pierce all of the beads, and bake them at 300°F (149°C) for about eight minutes.

9. After all of the pieces have cooled, embellish them with the metallic paints. Apply a small amount of Royal Ruby paint to the stiff-bristled brush, and stroke most of the paint onto a paper towel. Dry-brush scant amounts of paint to the bottoms of the acorns and all of the leaves. Using the same technique, apply the gold paint to the tops of the acorns.

10. After the paint has dried, thread your beads onto the monofilament or tigertail. Start with 14 of the smaller clay beads, alternating the polymer beads with the glass seed beads. Then add the following sequence of clay beads: one large, one small, one large, one small, two large, and one small (always alternating each polymer bead with a seed bead). Carefully add the pectoral piece; then string the remaining beads in the reverse order. Finish the ends with crimp beads, and add your clasp.

11. Complete the ensemble by attaching the earring backs with glue.

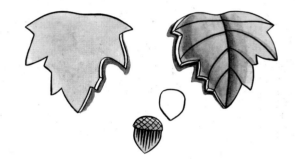

Figure 1

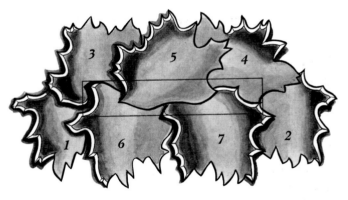

Figure 2

Figure 3

A TOUCH OF GOLD ———————

Byzantine Beauty
————————

Materials

*1-1/2 yard (1.4 m) 1/8-inch
  (3 mm) gold braid cord
1/4 yard (23 cm) long, white
  fringe
glue
1/2 block metallic copper
  Sculpey III
2 blocks white Sculpey III
gold leaf liquid paint
1 sheet metallic leaf
wooden shish-kebab skewers*

Tools

*rolling tool
craft knife*

Instructions

1. Start your necklace by making the tassel. Roll the fringe in a spiral, stopping to leave the last 2 inches (5 cm) free. Cut a piece of braid about 8 inches (20.3 cm) long, and glue the ends to the opposite sides of the top of the tassel. Then roll the remainder of the fringe over the ends of the braid. Glue the end of the fringe. (Refer to Figure 1.) Hint: Lightly wet the fringe to straighten the strands; then trim any uneven ends with scissors.

2. To make the barrel for the tassel, flatten the copper clay into a long, rectangular sheet. Using any ornament with deep indentations, incise a textural pattern into the sheet. With your fingers, shape the clay into a hollow barrel, making the inside diameter just large enough to make a snug fit for the tassel.

3. Bake the barrel at 230°F (110°C) for 15 to 25 minutes.

4. After it has cooled, apply gold leaf paint to the barrel. Make sure you are in a well-ventilated area while using this paint. Once the paint has dried thoroughly, insert the tassel into the barrel. Position the tassel so that its spiral top is recessed a bit from the top of the barrel, and glue the edges of the tassel to the inside of the barrel.

5. To make the tubular beads, flatten the white clay into a rectangular sheet about 1/2 inch (1.3 cm) thick. Place irregularly shaped strips of metallic leaf on top, and continue to flatten the clay until it is about 1/8 inch (3 mm) thick. The metallic leaf will break apart as the clay expands.

6. With your craft knife, cut the clay into a rectangle nearly as long as your wooden skewers. Lay two skewers close together near one long edge of the clay. Then roll the clay around the skewers. The

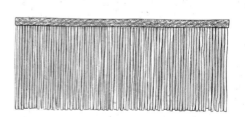

Figure 1

skewers define the shape of the hole and help make the tubes uniform in shape and size. If you want thin-walled tubes, cut the clay where it starts to overlap. For thicker walls, wrap the clay around the skewers more than once.

7. When you're satisfied with the shape, score the clay at the desired lengths for the tubes. This necklace uses two beads 2-1/4 inches (5.7 cm) long, three that are 3 inches (7.6 cm) long, and one that is 3-1/2 inches (8.9 cm) long. Most likely, you'll need to construct more than one batch of tubes on your skewers to result in enough beads.

8. Cut through the clay all around, and carefully remove the skewers from the tubes. Complete the round shape of the hole by sliding the skewers back and forth through the tubes. Once you have all of your tubes complete, use your fingers to gently shape them into curved beads. The longest bead is strung together with one midsize bead; shape these two so they fit well together.

9. Once you have the beads exactly as you like them, bake them at 230°F (110°C) for about 15 minutes. White clay can be very sensitive; check your beads for doneness, and don't let them burn.

10. To assemble the necklace, cut 14 inches (35.6 cm) of gold braid, and make a loop about 1-1/2 inches (3.8 cm) long at one end. String a midsize bead on the braid next to the loop, tie a double knot, and add one of the shortest tubes. Then tie a loose, temporary knot to hold the second bead onto the braid. Next, cut another 21 inches (53.3 cm) of braid, making an identical loop at one end. To this second, longer braid, add one midsize bead, one double knot, one short bead, and another double knot. Untie the temporary knot on the first length of braid, and tie the two pieces of braid together next to the short bead, adjusting the length in order to fit the necklace over your head. Then trim the braid close to the knot so the ends don't show.

11. Use the remaining braid to attach the last two tubes. String one bead, carry the braid through the loop on one side of the necklace, and tie a knot. Doubling back, add the last bead, carry the end through the other loop, and tie a knot. Finish by attaching the tassel to the double tubes in the center with a slip knot. (Refer to the photo for shaping.)

Egyptian Queen

Materials

1/4 block fresh, white polymer clay (any brand)
piece of clean, white paper
1/4 block of complementary color polymer clay for backing
1/8 block black clay
small amounts of red, light blue, ochre, turquoise, magenta, and fluorescent pink clay
small piece of metallic leaf
pin back
glue

Tools

rolling tool
burnisher or dull, flat instrument
craft knife

Instructions

1. Start by creating the central image. Use a color copier (set at 48%) to reproduce the gift paper shown here, or choose any other design you like. Any color copier will do; just make sure the toner is fresh when you use it.

2. Take a piece of fresh, white clay, and flatten it into a sheet approximately 1/8 inch (3 mm) thick. On the top surface of the clay, place a piece of clean, white paper. If you leave this on overnight, it will leach out any excess oils. Then

cut the clay into the shape you'd like for your pin. This one is a long rectangle with a rounded bottom.

3. Make a backing sheet for your pin using clay that blends well with the image. Flatten it into a sheet of equal thickness—about 1/8 inch (3 mm)—and somewhat larger in size than your piece of white clay. Center the white clay onto the backing sheet, gently pressing the two together to remove any air bubbles. Then cut the backing sheet the same shape as the image piece, leaving enough room to add the border.

4. Transfer the image by laying the copy face down onto the white clay. You may find it easier to handle your image if you trim it until it is close in size to your piece of clay. To enhance the transfer, gently rub the entire surface with a bur-nisher, a dull letter opener, or other similar tool. Then leave the piece undisturbed for 15 to 30 minutes. You can check the transfer for "done-ness" by lifting one corner. If it is too pale, let it sit another 30 minutes or so. Don't leave it too long, though, or the image may blur.

5. To make the gilded frame, roll a log of black clay long enough to encircle the outer edges of the pin. With your roller, slightly flatten the top surface of the log. Place long strips of metallic leaf on top of the clay, and continue rolling until you have reduced the thickness until it is equal to that of the white clay. The gold leaf will break into abstract shapes as it is stretched. Wrap the black frame around the image, press-ing it onto the backing sheet. Any excess that overhangs the backing sheet can be trimmed with your knife.

6. Create some decorative scrolls for the frame by making simple canes. The designs on each side are half slices from red and black bull's-eye canes. For the patterns at the top, make a simple jellyroll using light blue and ochre. A cluster of four scrolls at the bottom are made using a turquoise log wrapped in black, divided in two, and rolled together with a few highlights of magenta and fluorescent pink on one side. A light blue log wrapped in red and turquoise forms the pattern at the bottom center. Cut tis-sue-thin slices of these, together with some solid colors, and apply them around the frame, press-ing them into the frame.

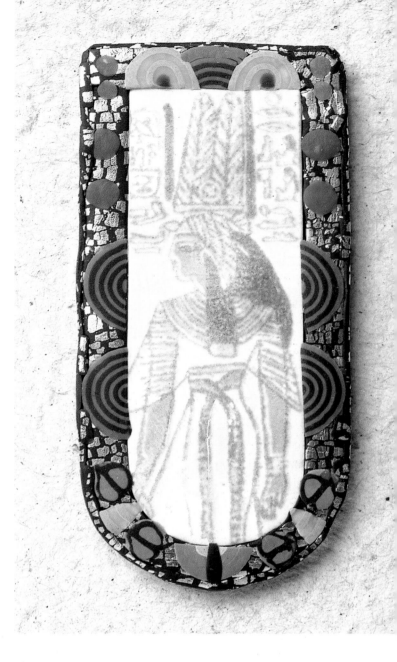

7. Bake the pin according to the manufacturer's recommendations for time and temperature.

8. When the piece has cooled, glue the pin back in place.

Cascade of Gold

Materials

1/4 block turquoise FIMO
1/4 block purple FIMO
wax paper
metallic leaf
*approximately 1-1/4 yard
  (1.1 m) fine-gauge gold
  chain*
pin back
glue

Tools

rolling tool
latex examination gloves
*wallpaper scraper or tis-
  sue-slicing blade*
toothpick
knitting needle (optional)

Instructions

1. Using a total of about 1/2 block of clay, marble two or three colors together. When you have a pattern you like, flatten the clay into a sheet about 1/4 inch (6 mm) thick. For this project, it is easier to handle the material if you flatten the clay on a sheet of wax paper.

2. Place a sheet of metallic leaf on the surface of the clay, rubbing your fingers over the leaf to make it adhere to the clay. (Because the leaf tarnishes easily, it is recommended that you wear gloves when handling it.) Remove any excess leaf from around the edges. Then continue flattening the sheet until it is as thin as you can comfortably handle it. (It should feel like a piece of fine leather—light and supple.) As the clay expands, the metallic leaf will crack, exposing the marbled clay underneath.

3. Cut the clay into two square pieces about 4 to 5 inches (10.2 to 12.7 cm) on each side (or the length of your blade, if possible). Set aside one piece, and cut the other one into strips about 1/8 inch (3 mm) wide. It is easier to cut perfect strips by pressing the entire length of the blade down at once, making sure to cut all the way to both ends of the sheet. As you cut them, don't pick up the strips; they should remain on the wax paper in their original position.

4. Turn the strips so they are oriented vertically, and with the side of your thumb, press along the top edge of the strips to make them adhere to the wax paper. Place another sheet of wax paper (about the size of your weaving square) at the top of the square, overlapping the clay by about 1/2 inch (1.3 cm). This sheet is used to keep the individual strips from sticking to the work as it is woven.

5. Count the number of strips and find the center one. If you have an even number of strips, remove one. With a toothpick, lift the bottom edge of the strip that is directly left of the center one. Carefully pick up the strip, and flip it over in a gentle curve so the top of the strip now touches the wax paper. Don't pull the strip too hard or press a crease into it. Repeat with the strip directly right of the center one.

6. Cut your first piece of chain so that it is long enough to cross all three center strips and have some to hang down on either side—about 4 inches (10.2 cm). Lay the piece of chain across the entire width of the strips; then lower the two raised strips back into their original positions. Congratulations. You've finished the first (bottom) row of the pin.

7. Now raise the center strip. Moving to the left, skip the strip you previously raised, and raise the one next to it. Then do the same on the right side. You should now have three strips raised and flipped over. Cut another piece of chain a little longer than the first (about 4-1/2 inches or 11.4 cm). Lay it across the lowered strips, and lower the three raised strips one at a time, moving from one side to the other.

8. For the third row, raise a total of four strips, again alternating in a checkerboard fashion from the strips raised in the previous row (see Figure 1). Cut the next piece of chain a little longer than the previous one, and lay it across the entire width of the strips. Remember to pull the wax paper down as you progress with your weaving to keep the strips from sticking to the weaving.

9. Each new row uses one more strip than the previous one, and the pin begins to take on its triangular shape. Continue the process until the piece is as large as you'd like or until you run out of strips to weave. Then set the weaving aside.

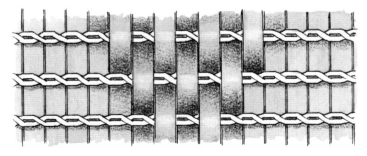

Figure 1

10. Remove the second square sheet of clay from its piece of wax paper, turn it upside-down, and place it metallic side down on the wax paper. Pick up the woven piece, and turn it over into the palm of your hand. Then slowly peel off the wax paper. Turning the weaving face up, place it onto the second sheet.

11. Now cut a piece of wax paper the size and shape (triangular) of the woven area, and place it on top of the weaving. Lift the chains from one side of the weaving, placing them onto the wax paper. Following the line formed by the chains, use your blade to cut away both layers of unwoven material. Repeat on the other side of the weaving. Then trim off any unwanted or uneven portions at the top or bottom.

12. With the entire piece in hand, press the woven strips to the backing gently enough not to distort the thickness of the strips. To smooth the edges, use the side of a knitting needle or toothpick.

13. Bake the pin at 250°F (120°C) for 20 to 30 minutes.

14. When the piece is cool, attach a pin back with glue.

MOLDED FORMS

Rising Sun

Materials

enough scrap clay to make a
  mold (see below)
1/4 block turquoise brilliant
  Sculpey III
small amounts of black and
  red Sculpey III
talcum powder
gold buffing compound
pin back
glue

Tools

small face (doll, Christmas
  ornament, etc.) for
  molding
small paintbrush
rolling tool
textured surface (shell,
  fan, or other)
craft knife

Instructions

1. Begin by selecting a small face—or something else—you'd like to mold. Small oriental statues, cherubs, and dolls are some possibilities for faces. For other interesting moldable items, look at antique iron work, wood carvings, or the bottoms of your sneakers. Once you've made your choice, brush a small amount of talcum powder onto the surface of the item to be molded. Take a ball of clay two or three times the size of the face or other item, and press it onto your object. Make sure to push the clay into any small crevices. (See pages 32–33 for more details on making molds.)

2. Carefully remove the clay from your object. Then bake the mold at 200°F (93°C) for about 50 minutes.

3. When the mold has cooled, roll your black clay into a teardrop shape. Place the pointed end into the nose cavity (or any other deep impression in your mold), and press the rest of the clay evenly into the mold. After smoothing the back, remove the soft clay from the mold.

4. To make the background pieces, divide the turquoise material into two segments 1/3 and 2/3 the total. Flatten these into irregularly shaped sheets about 1/4 inch (6 mm) thick. With each sheet laid onto a textured surface, use your roller to impress the texture onto the sheet. Make a similar piece using the red clay. If the three background sheets are not shaped the way you'd like, trim them with a craft knife. Then join all three in a pleasing arrangement, placing your molded face or other item on top.

5. Bake the completed pin for 30 to 40 minutes at 200°F (93°C).

6. When the pin has cooled, apply the buffing compound to each element. As a final step, glue on the finding.

Carved in Stone

Materials

1 block transparent FIMO
1/2 block turquoise FIMO
1-1/2 blocks nightglow
  FIMO
1 block black FIMO
small amounts of ochre and
  yellow FIMO
1 sheet variegated composition metallic leaf
talcum powder
dark brown or earth-tone
  acrylic paint
miscellaneous beads from old
  jewelry (optional)
black or white round elastic
glue

Tools

small electric chopper
  (optional, and don't use
  for food afterward)
slicing blade
doll's face 1 to 1-1/4 inch
  (2.5 to 3.2 cm) high
rolling tool
wooden modelling tool,
  flat with pointed end
metal skewer or coat
  hanger
1/2-inch (1.3 cm) hole
  cutter (brass tubing
  works well)
soft brush
#4/0 steel wool

Instructions

1. Unlike most projects, this one calls for some clay not to be conditioned beforehand. Using an electric chopper or a single-edge slicing blade, chop (do not mix) 1/2 block of turquoise and 1/2 block nightglow. Keep each color separate, and store the chopped pieces in plastic bags until ready to use. Then mix 1/4 block transparent with a 1/2-inch (1.3 cm) ball of ochre to make gold clay. Make pale yellow by mixing 1/4 block of transparent with a 1/4-inch (6 mm) ball of yellow and a 1/4- to 1/2-inch (6 mm to 1.3 cm) ball of ochre.

2. To make the press mold, make a pad of clay using about 1/4 block of the nightglow (or scrap material). After brushing powder lightly on the doll's face, press the clay onto the face, working from the center outward. Gently remove the pad, reshape it if necessary, and bake the mold at 265°F (130°C) for about 30 minutes.

3. When the mold has cooled, mix the clay for the face. Add one pea-sized ball of gold clay (from step 1) to about 1/4 block of nightglow. Use more clay than needed to fill the mold. Before inserting the clay into the mold, apply some powder to the mold. Roll the clay into an egg shape, and press the longer end into the nose cavity. Fill the mold with clay, and trim the excess off the back. Using the modelling tool to assist, ease the face out of the mold. Don't worry about any irregularities around the edges; they will be covered later. Set the face aside to rest.

4. To construct the irregular cane from which the beads are made, you'll need these components:

   #1: Flatten the gold clay into two equal-sized square sheets.

   #2: Repeat with the yellow clay, making the squares equal in size to #1.

   #3: Repeat with approximately 1/2 block of nightglow clay.

   #4: Repeat with 1/2 block of black clay.

   #5: Flatten 1/2 block of transparent clay into a rectangular sheet. Then put the metallic leaf on top, and use your roller to make the leaf adhere to the clay. Continue rolling to stretch the clay (and crack the leaf) until it is about 1/16 inch (1.6 mm) thick. Cut a strip about 1/2 by 3-1/2 inches (1.3 by 8.9 cm) to use later for cutting small circles. Cut the remaining sheet into four square pieces the same size as #1-4 above.

5. Assemble the irregular cane from the bottom up. (Figure 1 should help you visualize its construction.) The final effect of the cane is to resemble a stratified rock or mineral. Use your imagination, and enjoy the process. Start and finish with one sheet of #3. For the layers in between, sprinkle on some unconditioned, chopped bits of nightglow clay, and add full sheets or strips cut from the various colors prepared above. Place the sheets not just as flat layers: bunch them, wedge them, and make convoluted shapes. Fill in the gaps or make entire layers with bits of nightglow and turquoise clay. When you have an interesting composition, compress the cane first with your hands, then with a roller to increase the convolutions in the layers and to form a solid block. Then reduce the final cane to a diameter of about 1-1/2 inch (3.8 cm).

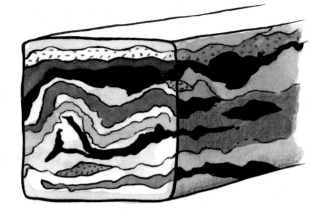

Figure 1

6. Trim off the front cross section, setting it aside for the smaller beads. Then cut a slice 1/8 inch (3 mm) thick, and place it on the back of the molded face. Bring the edges of the slice around the molded clay face, shawl-like, and lightly compress the edges without distorting the face. Use your skewer to pierce a hole through the edges behind the face.

7. Now cut a slab 1/2 inch (1.3 cm) thick from the irregular cane. From this piece cut three 1/2-inch (1.3 cm) cubes. Pierce two diagonally (beads labelled #1 in Figure 2), and facet the third by slicing off the edges (to make bead #2).

8. Cut the balance of the slab from the previous step in half, making two pieces each 1/2 inch (1.3 cm) by 1/2 inch (1.3 cm) by about 1 inch (2.5 cm) long. Cut the pieces so they are generally striped along their length. Then gently roll each into a log with a diameter slightly larger than 1/2 inch (1.3 cm), and trim each one to 1 inch (2.5 cm) long. Cut four 1/2-inch (1.3 cm)

Figure 2

circles from the reserved strip of combination #5 (from step 4). Use these to cap the ends of each log, and roll the ends on your work surface to create rounded domes. Shape each bead by lightly rolling it in the center to give it a somewhat curved hourglass shape. Pierce the beads (#3 in Figure 2) lengthwise with the skewer.

9. Make at least three round beads from scraps, varying them in size from 1/2 inch (1.3 cm) in diameter to one very small one flattened to form a spacer (beads marked #4). One of the beads in the photo contains a slice from a sunshine cane. If this is too ambitious, use another favorite cane or opt for random patterns crafted from scraps. Use the skewer to make holes, making one large enough to accommodate the knot of the elastic.

10. For the last two beads (#5), make two doughnut shapes from scraps.

11. Bake all of the beads, including the face, at 265°F (130°C) for about 45 minutes.

12. When the face bead has cooled, lightly brush brown acrylic paint over the whole face. Before it dries, wipe the color off the surface with a paper towel, leaving some brown in the crevices. After it has dried completely, use super-fine #4/0 steel wool to refine the face to your satisfaction. Then buff it to a soft shine with a towel.

13. Beginning with the bead with the larger hole, assemble all of the beads on the elastic. Adjust the length to fit, and tie an overhand knot. Before concealing the knot inside the bead, add a small dollop of glue just in case.

COLLAGE

Memories

Materials

1 block black Sculpey III
1 block white Sculpey III
1 block blue Sculpey III
1 block green Sculpey III
star stud
pin back
2 earring backs
glue

Tools

miniature, ornate picture frame
slicing blade
rolling tool (optional)
heart-shaped aspic cutter
another ornate textured surface

Instructions

1. To make a mold of a miniature, ornate picture frame, press a small slab of scrap clay onto the frame firmly and evenly. Remove the mold, and bake it at 275°F (135°C) for about 15 minutes.

2. When the mold has cooled, press a thick log of black clay firmly and evenly into the indentations in the mold. Remove the clay, trimming off any excess around the edges. Then place the star stud into the top center.

3. For the checkerboards, you can make either a short cane or a checkerboard sheet. To do the latter, start with one rectangular sheet of black and one of white, each at least as large as you want your earrings. (This pair is about 1 inch or 2.5 cm square, not including the ruffle.) Cut each sheet lengthwise into three strips, each about 1/8 inch (3 mm) wide. Reassemble the strips into a single sheet, but alternate the colors. Then cut the assembled sheet horizontally into eight short strips. Flip every other row to attain the checkerboard pattern. When it is satisfactory, press all of the pieces together. One or two passes with a roller may be needed to even the sheet when you're done.

4. Now cut the checkerboard into two equal squares the size you want for your earrings. Using the aspic cutter, remove a heart shape from the center of each checkerboard sheet, reserving one heart shape to use on the pin.

5. Bake both checkerboards and the frame for about 15 minutes at 275°F (135°C).

6. Now make a log about 1/4 inch (6 mm) in diameter from the blue clay. Flatten this into a long rectangular sheet about 1/16 inch (1.6 mm) thick, and gather the sheet into ruffles as if it were fabric. Wrap the ruffled sheet around the inside of the black frame and along one outside edge of each checkerboard frame. Press the soft clay to the harder frames to make it adhere.

7. Using a combination of blue, green, and white, mix a small amount of light turquoise clay. Flatten this into a sheet about 1/16 inch (1.6 mm) thick, and press the sheet onto an antique metal box or other ornate, textured surface. Then cut the turquoise sheet into three pieces identical in size to the two checkerboard earrings and the black frame pin. Press these pieces from behind to fill the centers of all three frames with the textured patterns. Place the reserved checkerboard heart into the center of the textured turquoise clay in the pin.

8. Bake all three pieces again for about 15 minutes at 275°F (135°C).

9. Use glue to attach the pin and earring backs.

Day at the Beach

Materials

previously prepared face
canes
several simple canes of
various colors and patterns
flesh-colored clay to match the
skin of your face canes
small amounts of bronze,
white, and blue Sculpey III
tracing vellum
parchment paper
barrette clip
glue

Tools

rolling tool
slicing blade
spoon

Instructions

1. Construct one, two, or three female face canes according to the procedures described on pages 29–30. You can obtain significant variation among your people just by changing their hair styles and body shapes, but if you enjoy making face canes, here is a perfect opportunity to show off your talents. Make one distinctly male face for the father figure, and substitute yellow clay for flesh to make a jolly old Sol. Reduce each cane to a size appropriate for the figures you want to place on the beach.

2. Mix the clay for the sand by combining a small amount of white clay with some bronze. Roll each color into a log; then twist and fold them together several times. Stop mixing before the color becomes uniform, leaving gentle grada-tions of tone. Repeat the process using blue and white for the sea/sky. Then, placing a log of sand clay next to one of sea/sky, flatten them together into a thick sheet. Cut the background slightly larger than the size you want for the finished barrette. After trimming, the clay should overhang the metal back by about 1/4 inch (6 mm) on both sides and at each end.

3. Construct the beach scene by making a collage of tissue-thin cane slices pressed onto the back-ground surface. When you first position the

figures, place them lightly onto the background. If you find you don't like their placement, use the edge of your blade to lift the cane slices off the background. Then smooth the background with your finger or roller.

4. Begin by placing the faces into position. Where two figures are close together, don't forget to leave room for their hair, which is a raucous assembly of geometric shapes taken from various canes. These characters have hair made from triangular canes, bars of alternating colors, and half-circles of abstract patterns. You could easily substitute tiny curls from a garlic press, thin strips of clay, or other methods you devise.

5. Next construct the bodies. Form simplified dresses by clustering several small cane slices into square or triangular shapes. The intended effect is playful, not realistic. Similarly, shape a rough T-shirt and shorts for your mustached fellow. Roll fine threads of flesh-colored clay to make the arms and legs of the figures, and flatten them in place.

6. Use slices from an abstract black and white cane to construct the family pet. There is no need to build a dog-shaped cane; simply cut slices, trim them into appropriate shapes for ears, head, legs, body, and tail. Then press them together onto the background. When compressed, any joints will become invisible.

7. Place the sun up in one corner, and add a few toys and beach litter for extra color.

8. Once you have your scene exactly as you want it, cover the collage with a sheet of tracing vellum. Use the bowl of a spoon to burnish the clay, smoothing the applied clay into the background. Then trim the landscape to size.

9. Finally, slice the finished landscape completely through the clay at 1/4- to 3/8-inch (6 mm to 1 cm) intervals. This will give the barrette more flexibility. Without handling the slices, slide them onto a piece of oven parchment. When the oven has preheated to 300°F (149°C), place the slices in the oven, and turn off the controls. Let them bake for about 30 minutes, checking periodically to make sure they don't burn.

10. Using a flexible glue such as E-6000, attach the cooled slices to the surface of the barrette clip.

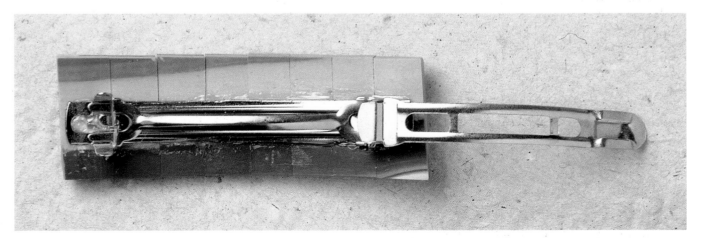

Tender Heart

Materials

small amounts of black, red,
  white, and blue Sculpey III
silver metallic powder
pin back
glue

Tools

rolling tool
craft knife
piece of lace or other
  textured fabric
small paintbrush

Instructions

1. Form a grape-sized piece of black clay into a heart with your hands, and gently flatten it. Alternatively, you could flatten the clay into a sheet and cut it into a heart shape with your craft knife.

2. Using your roller, press a piece of lace onto the clay to create a strong texture. Remove the lace, and dust the surface lightly with the metallic powder. Use your paintbrush, not your fingers, to apply the metallic powder.

3. To make the rosette, start with a small log of red clay. Flatten this into a long, rectangular sheet about 1/16 inch (1.6 mm) thick, and gather it into a ruffled spiral.

4. Mix a small amount of red clay with white, and add a pinch of blue to make a cool pink color. Roll the pink clay into a log about 1/4 inch (6 mm) in diameter; then flatten the log into a long rectangular sheet. Gather the sheet into ruffles, and attach it to the back of the heart, flaring the ruffles outward.

5. Similarly, make a blue ruffle, and attach it along the bottom of the heart. Mix a bit of pink clay with some blue to make purple, and form a third ruffle to lay behind the other two. Now place the rosette in an appropriate spot along the ruffled edge.

6. When you're satisfied with the design, bake the pin for about 15 minutes at 275°F (135°C).

7. When the piece has cooled, attach the pin back with glue.

Classical Monument

Materials

*scraps of any color polymer
clay totaling about 1-2
blocks*
*assortment of premade canes:
millefiore designs, stripes,
chevrons, others*
1 block black clay
*small amounts of metallic
dark green and metallic
purple clay*
artificial gold leaf
glue
pin back
clear acrylic gloss
gold buffing compound

Tools

rolling tool
slicing blade
craft knife
fine paintbrush
*parchment or heavy
tracing paper*
plastic hair comb

Instructions

1. Make the base for the brooch by flattening scrap clay into a sheet at least 1/8 inch (3 mm) thick. Cut slices as thin as you possibly can from a selection of colorful canes, arranging them on your thick slab of clay to form a collage at least as large as you'd like for the finished piece. Butt the slices against each other, overlap them, or put smaller ones on top of larger ones. For example, in this brooch, the cloud shapes are placed on top of a large slice of blue stripes, while the square and rectangular slices are butted against each other. (Note: the cane format for the clouds is irregular—see Figure 1—and each slice is cloud-shaped.)

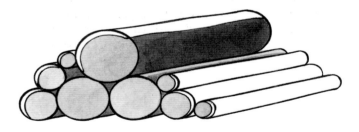

Figure 1

140

2. After placing the collage between two sheets of parchment paper, gently but firmly compress the slices and the slab together with your roller.

3. To apply gold leaf to your design, flatten a small amount of black (or any other dark color) clay until it is as thin as you can comfortably handle it. Place a sheet of metallic leaf on top, and roll again until fine cracks appear in the gold. With a craft knife, cut some strips of the gilded clay, and arrange them on your collage to separate the patterns or enhance the design. To make a design similar to this brooch, place a square of gold in the center of your collage. Then cut a smaller square hole in the center to make a window. Cut through the slab underneath, and remove the entire square.

4. When the design is satisfactory, use your craft knife to trim off any excess slab from your arrangement, and cut it into the form of a simple house. Place the collage on your baking surface, and form a tent of aluminum foil over the clay. Then bake the collage according to the clay manufacturer's guidelines.

5. To make the pillars on each side of the brooch, roll about 3/4 block of scrap clay into a thick log. Cut some very thin lengthwise slices from a striped loaf, and wrap these around the log so the stripes run the length of the log. Reduce the cane—and cut it when its length becomes unmanageable—until it is close to the diameter you want. Then move your hands in opposite directions as you roll the log to cause the stripes to spiral. Alternate twisting and rolling until the cane is finely twisted and appropriate in size for your design. Cut two equal lengths, and press them onto the sides of your baked base.

6. For the capitals, roll two pieces of clay into round balls comparable in diameter to the columns. Place a thin slice from a face cane or other design on each ball. After compressing the slices into the clay, position each ball on top of a pillar.

7. Begin the roof by rolling a small amount of black clay into a log less than 1/4 inch (6 mm) in diameter. Then flatten it into a narrow strip about 1/8 inch (3 mm) thick. Follow the same process with some metallic green clay, but make this strip slightly thicker and wider. Lay the black strip—thin edge facing outward—along the roof edges, and trim it to fit between the two capitals. At the peak, make a miter cut for a clean fit. To create a textural effect, press the teeth of a plastic comb into the edge of the

black clay. Now take the wider strip of green clay, and place it on top of the black strip, mitering the top joint and bottom edges.

8. Make a third strip from a small amount of metallic purple clay. Cut the strip so that it measures about 2 inches (5.1 cm) longer than the width of the house (not including the pillars). Then roll each end into a spiral that just fits at the base of each pillar. You may need to trim the pillars a bit to accommodate the spirals. Impress the comb into this platform strip as you did on the roof.

9. To create a background scene in the window, flatten a very small piece of clay, and cut a square somewhat larger than the window opening. Using paper-thin slices from some favorite canes, create a scene you enjoy, and roll the slices onto the clay.

10. To add whimsy to your brooch, sculpt a torso to stand in the window. If this is too ambitious, find a small figure to mold. This brooch also includes a face and hand molded from some nativity figures. (For details on making press molds and molding, see pages 32–33.)

11. Bake all of the brooch elements at the recommended time and temperature, again tenting them with aluminum foil. The window scene and molded pieces can be baked separately and later glued.

12. Once the pieces have cooled, check to see if any of the architectural elements can be pulled off. If they can, apply a small amount of glue. Using the glue sparingly, mount the window scene behind its opening and the molded elements in place. Using a generous amount of glue, attach the pin back.

13. To finish the piece, apply a clear gloss acrylic over all areas treated with gold leaf. Then, with your finger, apply gold buffing compound on the roof and textured platform areas and on the molded pieces. Carefully glue the molded pieces in place, and your brooch is complete.

GLOSSARY

Cane: Logs of various shapes and sheets of clay are joined together to make a cane, which shows its pattern when viewed from the end. Once the distorted ends are removed, each slice cut from the cane contains the same exact pattern as every other slice.

Loaf: Another word for a cane, usually one that is square or rectangular.

Log: Also called a snake or rod, this is a solid, cylindrical piece of polymer clay.

Millefiore (plural, *millefiori*): A term coined by Italian glass makers—literally translated as "thousand flowers"—for their work containing numerous tiny patterns resembling flowers (often found in paperweights and other art objects made of glass). This term has more recently been adopted by polymer clay artists to describe their work, which employs the same basic cane making techniques used byglass makers.

Piercing tool: Any item capable of making a hole through unbaked polymer clay.

Reducing: The act of reducing the size of the image in a cane. This is achieved by rolling a cylindrical cane or by pinching and pulling a square or triangular cane. In the process, the cane itself lengthens, but the pattern elements retain their distinct color and position.

Roller: A tool, such as a rolling pin, glass, or brayer, used for flattening polymer clay into sheets.

Slicing blade: A sharp, single-edged blade used to cut slices of various thicknesses from polymer clay.

A necklace "sampler," including beads made from several canes, by Tamela Wells.

ACKNOWLEDGMENTS

Many thanks to…

URSULA BENNETT at T & F Kunststoffe, the producers of Cernit, for providing technical and historical information.

IRENE DEAN for providing technical advice and recommendations and for graciously lending equipment for photography purposes.

A.D. DIMMEL at Eberhard Faber, the makers of FIMO, who patiently and thoroughly answered many letters and facsimiles requesting information on their products.

SUSAN KINNEY for the many hours she devoted to the beautiful handmade papers that fill this book.

BARRY OLEN at Beads and Beyond in Asheville, North Carolina, for sharing some of his extensive knowledge of beads and jewelry making and for his generous loan of jewelry making tools.

HOPE PHILLIPS at Polyform Products Company, the manufacturers of Pro-Mat and Sculpey products, for answering questions and providing technical information.

HOWARD SEGAL at The Clay Factory in Escondido, California, a wonderful source for a variety of polymer clays, tools, and supplies, for seeking answers to some difficult questions.

JOY ZUKE of Fairbanks, Alaska, for lending her triangular woven pin, created by Thessaly Barnett and shown on page 129, for use in this book.

JENNIFER BOURGEOIS at Jewelry Design in Asheville, North Carolina, for her kind loan of jewelry making tools.

"As happy as a pig in clover," by Marguerite Kuhl and Jane Vislocky.

BIBLIOGRAPHY

Allen, Jamey D. "Millefiori Polyform Techniques." *Ornament* 12 (Summer 1989): 46-49.

Carlson, Maureen. *FIMO Folk*. Canby, OR: Hot Off the Press, 1992.

Dustin, Kathleen. "The Use of Polyform in Bead-Making." *Ornament* 11 (Spring 1988): 16-19.

Eberhard Faber. *FIMO Ideas for Creative Modelling*. Neumarkt, Germany: self-published, 1988.

———. *New FIMO Modelling Ideas*. Neumarkt, Germany: self-published, 1986.

Edwards, David. *Using FIMO*. San Diego: self-published, 1990.

Gessert-Tschakert, Evelyn. *Modelling Fashionable Jewelry with FIMO*. Neumarkt, Germany: Eberhard Faber, 1987.

Harris, Elizabeth. *A Bead Primer*. Prescott, AZ: The Bead Museum, 1987.

Hjort, Barbara. "Buttons and Beads: Bake Your Own from Polymer Clay." *Threads* 39 February/March 1992): 58-61.

Jensen, Gay. "Discover Polymer Clay." *Shuttle Spindle & Dyepot* 22 (Winter 1990-91): 46-49.

National Polymer Clay Guild. *POLYinforMER* (newsletter published five times per year, starting January 1991). McLean, VA.

Poris, Ruth F. *Step-by-Step Bead Stringing*. Tampa: Golden Hands Press, 1984.

Roche, Nan. "Creating with Polymer." *Shuttle Spindle & Dyepot* 22 (Winter 1990-91): 52-53.

———. *The New Clay*. Rockville, MD: Flower Valley Press, 1991.

Ross, Anne L. "City Zen Cane." *Ornament* 15 (Winter 1991).

Rufener, Shirley. *Fancy FIMO Jewelry*. Canby, OR: Hot Off the Press, 1992.

INDEX

Molded face by Kathleen Amt.